T0075190

Explainable Agency in Artificial Intelligence

This book focuses on a subtopic of explainable AI (XAI) called *explainable agency (EA)*, which involves producing records of decisions made during an agent's reasoning, summarizing its behavior in human-accessible terms, and providing answers to questions about specific choices and the reasons for them. We distinguish explainable agency from interpretable machine learning (IML), another branch of XAI that focuses on providing insight (typically, for an ML expert) concerning a learned model and its decisions. In contrast, explainable agency typically involves a broader set of AI-enabled techniques, systems, and stakeholders (e.g., end users), where the explanations provided by EA agents are best evaluated in the context of human subject studies.

The chapters of this book explore the concept of endowing intelligent agents with explainable agency, which is crucial for agents to be trusted by humans in critical domains such as finance, self-driving vehicles, and military operations. This book presents the work of researchers from a variety of perspectives and describes challenges, recent research results, lessons learned from applications, and recommendations for future research directions in EA. The historical perspectives of explainable agency and the importance of interactivity in explainable systems are also discussed. Ultimately, this book aims to contribute to the successful partnership between humans and AI systems.

Features:

- Contributes to the topic of *explainable artificial intelligence* (XAI)
- Focuses on the XAI subtopic of *explainable agency*
- Includes an introductory chapter, a survey, and five other original contributions

Chapman & Hall/CRC Artificial Intelligence and Robotics Series

Series Editor: Roman Yampolskiy

Digital Afterlife and the Spiritual Realm
Maggi Savin-Baden

A First Course in Aerial Robots and Drones
Yasmina Bestaoui Sebbane

AI by Design: A Plan for Living with Artificial Intelligence
Catriona Campbell

The Global Politics of Artificial Intelligence
Edited by Maurizio Tinnirello

Unity in Embedded System Design and Robotics: A Step-by-Step Guide
Ata Jahangir Moshayedi, Amin Kolahdooz, Liao Liefa

Meaningful Futures with Robots: Designing a New Coexistence
Edited by Judith Dörrenbächer, Marc Hassenzahl, Robin Neuhaus, Ronda Ringfort-Felner

Topological Dynamics in Metamodel Discovery with Artificial Intelligence: From Biomedical to Cosmological Technologies
Ariel Fernández

A Robotic Framework for the Mobile Manipulator: Theory and Application
Nguyen Van Toan and Phan Bui Khoi

AI in and for Africa: A Humanist Perspective
Susan Brokensha, Eduan Kotzé, Burgert A. Senekal

Artificial Intelligence on Dark Matter and Dark Energy: Reverse Engineering of the Big Bang
Ariel Fernández

Explainable Agency in Artificial Intelligence: Research and Practice
Silvia Tulli and David W. Aha

For more information about this series please visit: https://www.routledge.com/Chapman--HallCRC-Artificial-Intelligence-and-Robotics-Series/book-series/ARTILRO

Explainable Agency in Artificial Intelligence

Research and Practice

Edited by

Silvia Tulli

David W. Aha

CRC Press is an imprint of the
Taylor & Francis Group, an **informa** business

First edition published 2024
by CRC Press
2385 NW Executive Center Drive, Suite 320, Boca Raton FL 33431

and by CRC Press
4 Park Square, Milton Park, Abingdon, Oxon, OX14 4RN

CRC Press is an imprint of Taylor & Francis Group, LLC

ISBN: 978-1-032-40913-9 (hbk)
ISBN: 978-1-032-39258-5 (pbk)
ISBN: 978-1-003-35528-1 (ebk)

DOI: 10.1201/9781003355281

Typeset in Minion
by MPS Limited, Dehradun

Contents

Preface

MOTIVATION

As artificial intelligence (AI) begins to impact our everyday lives as well as industry, government, and society at large with tangible consequences, it becomes increasingly important for practitioners and users to understand the reasons and models underlying an AI-enabled system's decisions and recommendations. Explainable agency captures the idea that AI systems will need to be trusted by humans and, as autonomous agents themselves, "must be able to explain their decisions and the reasoning that produced their choices" (Langley et al. 2017).

In contrast to the much broader topic of explainable AI (XAI), and its predominant focus on interpretable machine learning (IML), this book focuses on *explainable agency*. It addresses a gap in the literature on published volumes concerning this subtopic of XAI.

This book presents the work of researchers focused on different facets of explainable agency, from diverse backgrounds, and describes challenges, new directions, recent research results, and lessons from applications. It includes or references contributions from AI, human-computer interaction, human-robot interaction, cognitive science, human factors, and philosophy.

DEFINITION OF EXPLAINABLE AGENCY

Endowing agents with explainable agency is not only an academic exercise but a foremost priority in many real-world scenarios. In financial markets, self-driving vehicles, robot-assisted surgery, military operations, and other critical domains, whenever the behavior of these systems does not match human expectations (e.g., the car takes an unfamiliar turn), it is necessary to inform humans about how and why a certain decision has been taken. Providing these types of explanations impacts human trust towards the system (Doshi-Velez & Kim 2017; Gunning & Aha 2019; Kocielnik et al. 2019; Lipton 2018; Miller 2019) and contributes to creating a shared mental model among the human and the AI system, leading to a more successful human-AI partnership (Kamar et al. 2012; Zhang et al. 2021).

Given a set of objectives and the necessary background knowledge that is relevant to these objectives, to be explainable an intelligent agent should produce records of decisions made during its reasoning, summarize its behavior in human-accessible terms, and provide answers to questions about specific choices and the reasons for them (Langley 2019). Producing records of decisions made during planning should include stating the alternatives the agent considered, giving its reasons for selecting them over alternatives, and describing its expectations for each option (Zhang et al. 2015). The information provided by the agent needs to be expressed at different levels of abstraction as appropriate and clarify how the performed actions relate to inferences made by the agent. Explanations should be given especially in situations where actual events diverged from expectations and the agent had to adapt in response (Kulkarni et al. 2019). To ensure intelligibility, the information should be presented in terms of beliefs, goals, and activities that people find to be familiar (Miller 2017).

Since explainable agency is an attribute given by the observer inherently motivated by the human quest of understanding an agent's behavior, human judgments have a pivotal role in the evaluation process. Measures on the effectiveness of the explanations include the evaluation of mental representations of the inferential process that end users have of a given model (Hoffman et al. 2018; Vilone et al. 2021).

HISTORICAL PERSPECTIVES

During the infancy of intelligent systems, notions of explainable agency and the importance of being explainable to end-users began to be developed. Examples of early explainable systems are from critical domains like healthcare (Swartout et al. 1993). The XPLAIN system (Swartout et al. 1983, 1985), which attempted to provide generated explanations for an intelligent medical therapy program, is an early example of explainable agency used in practice. In addition to providing explanations of the system's goals, XPLAIN could also provide justifications. Other explainable methods in the medical domain aimed at strategic-level explanations (Hasling et al. 1984). Notably, these early examples of explainable agency in systems were focused on the end user and communicating explanations.

Interactivity played a central role in early explainable systems, and the importance of the user was highlighted in several research contributions. The impact of a user-centered explainable system on the end user was studied by Ye and Johnson (1995); they affirmed how such a facility can boost the user's confidence and attitude towards the system. To further provide more targeted explanations, attempts were also made to model the user's mental model, with different levels of abstraction (Chandrasekaran & Tanner 1989). Arguably, early work focused substantial attention on the user and interactive aspects of explainable systems, perhaps more so than in recent years.

An XAI winter followed this early time period that was characterized by a relative dearth of relevant research reported at major AI venues, although exceptions included efforts by some research groups (e.g., van Lent et al. 2004) and some meetings such as the series of *Explanation-aware Computing* (ExaCt) Symposia and Workshops (2005–2012). More recently, the advent of deep neural networks, their utility in critical applications, and their opaque models have driven an XAI resurgence. For example, this motivated DARPA's Explainable AI program (Gunning & Aha 2019; Gunning et al. 2021) and dozens of workshops and other events held annually at many AI conferences (e.g., IJCAI). While IML has received the vast majority of attention during this time period, research on explainable agency has also been increasingly pursued (e.g., Anjomshoae et al. 2019; Sado et al. 2023; Sreedharan et al. 2022). This motivated the *Explainable Agency in AI* Workshops held at the annual AAAI Conference on AI in 2021 and 2022, and led to this volume. The chapters in this book focus primarily on the explainable agency perspective of XAI.

CHAPTER SUMMARIES

Our book begins with Pat Langley's introductory chapter on explainable agency titled *From Explainable to Justified Agency*. In it, he provides motivations for studying explainable agents, frames the topic, discusses representational issues, and then presents three forms of self explanation (i.e., structural, preference, and process explanations), distinguishing them according to their abilities, and raising hypotheses concerning them. Pat then describes normative and justified agents, and how these relate to explainable agents (i.e., they describe their activities in reference to environment norms). This is an excellent introduction to explainable agents that frames and distinguishes this topic from research on interpretable machine learning.

Next, the chapter *A Survey of Global Explanations in Reinforcement Learning* by Yotam Amitai and Ofra Amir contributes to the field of explainable agency by reviewing research on global explanations for reinforcement learning (RL) agents. RL is increasingly deployed in real-world settings, and understanding the overall behavior, strategy, or reasoning of RL agents is crucial for explainable agency. Their chapter identifies three main types of global explanations proposed in the literature for RL agents, including interpretable representations of policies or the underlying Markov decision process, demonstrations of policy behavior, and rule-based methods using logical rules. The authors also discuss evaluation methods used to assess the contribution of global explanations, such as user studies, qualitative analyses, and quantitative measures. This chapter is unique in its focus on global explanations in RL, and it identifies emerging trends, gaps, and potential avenues for future research in this area.

In his chapter *Integrated Knowledge-Based Reasoning and Data-Driven Learning for Explainable Agency in Robotics*, Mohan Sridharan describes a robotics architecture that integrates model-based and data-driven methods to enable explainable agency. In doing so, it combines non-monotonic and probabilistic methods to reason at multiple abstraction levels, and interactive learning to provide on-demand explanations that describe its decisions and beliefs. Mohan describes an evaluation of this architecture on computer vision and planning tasks for robotic hand manipulation of interpreted objects, demonstrating its ability to answer factual and contrastive questions about its actions as well as temporally situated questions about its beliefs. This contribution is novel, in this volume, in its focus on a robotics architecture.

Ashok Goel, Vrinda Nandan, Eric Gregori, Sungeun An, and Spencer Rugaber's chapter *Explanation as Question Answering Based on User Guides* instead focuses on the importance for an explainable agent to leverage knowledge of its design and operation to answer user questions. Their use case concerns ecology, and specifically the Smithsonian Institution's Encyclopedia of Life (EoL). They describe how their AskJill question-answering agent employs EOL's user guide to answer users' questions during interaction with VERA, an AI-enabled interactive learning environment. In their human subjects evaluation, they found that AskJill performed admirably, answering 95% of user questions correctly among those within scope of its capabilities. This contribution is unique among this book's chapters in its focus on explanations concerning the design of an intelligent agent.

The chapter *Interpretable Multi-Agent Reinforcement Learning with Decision-Tree Policies* by Milani et al. focuses on interpreting and verifying policies learned from deep multi-agent reinforcement learning algorithms. It introduces two novel algorithms, IVIPER and MAVIPER, for learning interpretable decision-tree policies in multi-agent reinforcement learning. This chapter provides a comprehensive background on Markov games and multi-agent reinforcement learning algorithms, and presents experiments validating the effectiveness of the algorithms in producing high-quality decision-tree policies for coordination in cooperative environments.

Abhijeet Krishnan and Chris Martens's chapter *Towards the Automatic Synthesis of Interpretable Chess Tactics* focuses on an explainable agent that can describe a policy for playing chess. They describe a method for generating an interpretable policy that incorporates symbolic domain knowledge learned by an inductive logic programming system. They also describe a measure for tactic divergence and used it to evaluate a set of learned tactics. Their contribution is unique here due to its focus on improving interpretability of a reinforcement learning policy by incorporating domain knowledge of game-playing tactics.

Finally, the chapter *The Need for Empirical Evaluation of Explanation Quality* by Nicholas Halliwell, Fabien Gandon, Freddy Lecue, and Serena Villata contributes to the field of explainable agency by proposing and evaluating an approach to identify relevant features in the input space used by prototype networks, leveraging latent features learned by the model, with the goal of improving interpretability and understandability. It discusses the challenges of evaluating explanation quality without ground truth explanations and emphasizes the need for methods to generate explanations and compare their suitability.

FINAL REMARKS

This volume contains a selection of extended papers presented at the *Explainable Agency in Artificial Intelligence* workshops held in conjunction with the 2021 and 2022 AAAI Conferences on Artificial Intelligence. In addition, more recent contributions from the workshops' invited speakers have been added.

We would like to acknowledge the insightful exchanges we had with our collaborators, Mark Keane and Prashan Madumal, who co-organized the AAAI-22 workshop with us. Their contributions provided the foundation for this book and we are grateful for their partnership. Additionally, we would like to express our appreciation to all the authors who contributed to this book. Your insights, knowledge, and hard work were instrumental in creating this book. Thank you!

Silvia Tulli
Institut des systèmes intelligents et de robotique, Sorbonne University, Paris, France
David W. Aha
Navy Center for Applied Research in AI, Naval Research Laboratory, Washington, DC, USA

REFERENCES

Anjomshoae, S., Najjar, A., Calvaresi, D., & Främling, K. (2019). Explainable agents and robots: Results from a systematic literature review. *Proceedings of the Eighteenth International Conference on Autonomous Agents and Multiagent Systems* (pp. 1078–1088). Montreal, Canada: International Foundation for Autonomous Agents and Multiagent Systems.

Buijsman, S. (2023). Why and how should we explain AI? In M. Chetouani, V. Dignum, P. Lukowicz, & C. Sierra (Eds.), *Human-Centered Artificial Intelligence: Advanced Lectures* (pp. 196–215). Chambery, France: Springer International Publishing.

Cau, F. M., Hauptmann, H., Spano, L. D., & Tintarev, N. (2023). Supporting high-uncertainty decisions through AI and logic-style explanations. *Proceedings of the Twenty-Eighth International Conference on Intelligent User Interfaces* (pp. 251–263). New York, NY: ACM Press.

Chandrasekaran, B., & Tanner, M. (1989). Explaining control strategies in problem solving. *IEEE Intelligent Systems, 4*, 9–15.

Doshi-Velez, F., & Kim, B. (2017). Towards a rigorous science of interpretable machine learning. *arXiv preprint arXiv:1702.08608.*

Ehsan, U., Wintersberger, P., Liao, Q. V., Watkins, E. A., Manger, C., Daumé III, H., Riener, A., & Riedl, M. O. (2022). Human-centered explainable AI (HCXAI): Beyond opening the black-box of AI. *Extended Abstracts of the CHI Conference on Human Factors in Computing Systems* (pp. 1–7). New York, NY: ACM Press.

Gunning, D., & Aha, D. W. (2019). DARPA's explainable artificial intelligence program. *AI Magazine, 40*(2), 44–58.

Gunning, D., Vorm, E., Wang, Y., & Turek, M. (2021). DARPA's explainable AI (XAI) program: A retrospective. *Authorea Preprints.*

Gutiérrez, F., Htun, N. N., Abeele, V. V., De Croon, R., & Verbert, K. (2022). Explaining call recommendations in nursing homes: A user-centered design approach for interacting with knowledge-based health decision support systems. *Proceedings of the Twenty-Seventh International Conference on Intelligent User Interfaces* (pp. 162–172). Helsinki, Finland: ACM Press.

Hasling, D. W., Clancey, W. J., & Rennels, G. D. (1983). Strategic explanations for a diagnostic consultation system. *International Journal of Man-Machine Studies, 20*, 3–19.

Hoffman, R. R., Mueller, S. T., Klein, G., & Litman, J. (2018). Metrics for explainable AI: Challenges and prospects. *arXiv preprint arXiv:1812.04608.*

Kamar, E., Hacker, S., & Horvitz, E. (2012). Combining human and machine intelligence in large-scale crowdsourcing. *Proceedings of the Autonomous Agents and Multiagent Systems Conference* (pp. 467–474). Valencia, Spain: International Foundation for Autonomous Agents and Multiagent Systems.

Kulkarni, A., Zha, Y., Chakraborti, T., Vadlamudi, S. G., Zhang, Y., & Kambhampati, S. (2019). Explicable planning as minimizing distance from expected behavior. *Proceedings of the Eighteenth International Conference on Adaptive Agents and Multi-Agent Systems* (pp. 2075–2077). Montreal, Canada: International Foundation for Autonomous Agents and Multiagent Systems

Langley, P., Meadows, B., Sridharan, M., & Choi, D. (2017). Explainable agency for intelligent autonomous systems. *Proceedings of the Thirty-First AAAI Conference on Artificial Intelligence* (pp. 4762–4763). San Francisco, CA: AAAI Press.

Langley, P. (2019). Explainable, normative, and justified agency. *Proceedings of the Thirty-Third AAAI Conference on Artificial Intelligence* (pp. 9775–9779). Honolulu, HI: AAAI Press.

Liao, Q. V., Gruen, D., & Miller, S. (2020). Questioning the AI: Informing design practices for explainable AI user experiences. *Proceedings of the CHI Conference on Human Factors in Computing Systems* (pp. 1–15). Honolulu, HI: ACM Press.

Miller, T. (2019). Explanation in artificial intelligence: Insights from the social sciences. *Artificial Intelligence, 267*, 1–38.

Ooge, J., & Verbert, K. (2022). Explaining artificial intelligence with tailored interactive visualisations. In *Proceedings of the Twenty-Seventh International Conference on Intelligent User Interfaces.* Helsinki, Finland: ACM Press.

Pearl, J. (2000). *Models, reasoning and inference.* Cambridge, UK: Cambridge University Press.

Schoonderwoerd, T. A. J., Jorritsma, W., Neerincx, M. A., & Van Den Bosch, K. (2021). Human-centered XAI: Developing design patterns for explanations of clinical decision support systems. *International Journal of Human Computer Studies, 154*, 1–25.

Sado, F., Loo, C. K., Liew, W. S., Kerzel, M., & Wermter, S. (2023). Explainable goal-driven agents and robots: A comprehensive review. *ACM Computing Surveys, 55*(10), 1–41.

Sreedharan, S., Kulkarni, A., & Kambhampati, S. (2022). *Explainable human-AI interaction: A planning perspective*. Morgan and Claypool Publishers.

Swartout, W. R. (1983). XPLAIN: A system for creating and explaining expert consulting programs. *Artificial Intelligence, 21*(3), 285–325.

Swartout, W. R. (1985). Explaining and justifying expert consulting programs. In *Computer-assisted medical decision making* (pp. 254–271). New York, NY: Springer New York.

Swartout, W. R., & Moore, J. D. (1993). Explanation in second generation expert systems. In *Second Generation Expert Systems* (pp. 543–585). Springer Berlin Heidelberg.

Van Lent, M., Fisher, W., & Mancuso, M. (2004). An explainable artificial intelligence system for small-unit tactical behavior. *Proceedings of the Nineteenth National Conference on Artificial Intelligence* (pp. 900–907). San Jose, CA: AAAI Press.

Vilone, G., & Longo, L. (2021). Notions of explainability and evaluation approaches for explainable artificial intelligence. *Information Fusion, 76*, 89–106.

Waa, J., Nieuwburg, E., Cremers, A., & Neerincx, M. (2020). Evaluating XAI: A comparison of rule-based and example-based explanations. *Artificial Intelligence, 291*, 103404.

Ye, L. R., & Johnson, P. E. (1995). The impact of explanation facilities on user acceptance of expert systems advice. *Management Information Systems Quarterly, 19*, 157–172.

Zhang, Y., Zhuo, H., & Kambhampati, S. (2015). Plan explainability and predictability for cobots. *ArXiv, abs/1511.08158*.

Zhang, R., McNeese, N. J., Freeman, G., & Musick, G. (2021). An ideal human: Expectations of AI teammates in human-AI teaming. *Proceedings of the ACM Conference on Human-Computer Interaction* (pp. 1–25). ACM Press.

Editor Biographies

Dr. Silvia Tulli is an Assistant Professor at Sorbonne University. She received her Marie Curie ITN research fellowship and completed her Ph.D. at Instituto Superior Técnico. Her research interests lie at the intersection of explainable AI, interactive machine learning, and reinforcement learning. Silvia has co-organized multiple workshops around the themes of explainable AI at top conferences such as IJCAI, AAAI, ICAPS, and ICRA. Silvia's work has been showcased at conferences such as NeurIPS and AAAI, and recognized with various awards and scholarships, including the Best Student Paper Award at ICSR 2020.

Dr. David W. Aha (UC Irvine, 1990) serves as the Director of the AI Center at the Naval Research Laboratory in Washington, DC. His research interests include goal reasoning agents, deliberative autonomy, case-based reasoning, explainable AI, machine learning (ML), reproducible studies, and related topics. David launched the UCI Repository for ML Databases, served as a AAAI Councilor, co-created the AAAI Video Competition, received AAAI's Robert S. Engelmore Memorial Lecture Award, and received awards for five publications. He has led the evaluation teams for four DARPA programs and one ONR program.

Contributors

David W. Aha
Naval Research Laboratory
Washington, DC

Ofra Amir
Technion - Israel Institute of Technology
Haifa, Israel

Yotam Amitai
Technion - Israel Institute of Technology
Haifa, Israel

Sungeun An
Georgia Institute of Technology
Atlanta, GA

Fei Fang
Carnegie Mellon University
Pittsburgh, PA

Fabien Gandon
Inria, Université Côte d'Azur, and CNRS
Valbonne, France

Ashok Goel
Georgia Institute of Technology
Atlanta, GA

Eric Gregori
Georgia Institute of Technology
Atlanta, GA

Nicholas Halliwell
Inria, Université Côte d'Azur, and CNRS
Valbonne, France

Charles Kamhoua
Army Research Laboratory
Adelphi, MD

Abhijeet Krishnan
North Carolina State University
Raleigh, NC

Pat Langley
Stanford University
Stanford, CA
and
The Institute for the Study of Learning and Expertise
Palo Alto, CA

Freddy Lecue
Inria, Université Côte d'Azur, CNRS
Valbonne, France
and
CortAIx, Thales
Montreal, Canada

Chris Martens
North Carolina State University
Raleigh, NC

Stephanie Milani
Carnegie Mellon University
Pittsburgh, PA

Vrinda Nandan
Georgia Institute of Technology
Atlanta, GA

Evangelos E. Papalexakis
University of California
Riverside, CA

Spencer Rugaber
Georgia Institute of Technology
Atlanta, GA

Zheyuan Ryan Shi
Carnegie Mellon University
Pittsburgh, PA

Mohan Sridharan
University of Birmingham
Birmingham, UK

Nicholay Topin
Carnegie Mellon University
Pittsburgh, PA

Silvia Tulli
Sorbonne University
Paris, France

Serena Villata
Inria, Université Côte d'Azur, CNRS
Valbonne, France

Zhicheng Zhang
Carnegie Mellon University
Pittsburgh, PA
and
Army Research Laboratory
Adelphi, MD

CHAPTER 1

From Explainable to Justified Agency

Pat Langley

Center for Design Research, Stanford University, Stanford, USA; Institute for the Study of Learning and Expertise, Palo Alto, CA, USA

INTRODUCTION

Intelligent systems are becoming more widely adopted for critical tasks like driving cars and controlling military robots. Naturally, increased reliance on such devices has led to concerns about the interpretability of their complex behavior. Before people will fully trust such autonomous agents, they must be able to explain their decisions so that we can gain insight into their operation. There is now a substantial literature on explanation in systems that learn from experience, but it has focused on tasks like object recognition and reactive control, typically using opaque encodings of expertise that lend themselves only to shallow elucidation, as in 'heat maps' that display activation levels.

However, we also need research on explanation for more complex tasks that involve multi-step decision making, such as the generation and execution of plans. Approaches to these problems rely on high-level representations that are themselves easily interpreted, but challenges arise in communicating solutions that combine these elements and the reasons they were chosen. In this chapter, I focus on such settings. Some work on explanation, especially with opaque models, has dealt with post hoc rationalizations of behavior, rather than the actual reasons for it. In the pages that follow, I concentrate on the latter. Moreover, I will focus on *self explanations*, that is, the reasons the explaining agent carried out

DOI: 10.1201/9781003355281-1

certain activities. Elsewhere (Langley 2019), I have referred to this ability as *explainable agency.*[1]

We can specify the task of explainable agency in generic terms. Given domain knowledge for generating task solutions and criteria for evaluating candidates, the agent attempts to find one or more solutions. After generating, and possibly executing, these solutions, a human asks the agent to clarify its decisions, at which point it must share its reasoning in comprehensible terms. One example involves an intelligent robot that plans and executes a reconnaissance mission, after which it takes part in an 'after-action review' where it answers questions from a human supervisor. There has been some research on such *explainable planning* (Fox et al. 2017; Smith 2012; Zhang et al. 2017), but we need more effort devoted to this important topic.

In the sections that follow, I discuss different senses of the term 'explanation' and consider some factors that arise when representing such structures. Next, I discuss three types of self explanation, along with approaches to indexing, retrieving, and transmitting them. After this, I introduce the notion of *normative agency*, which takes social maxims into account during decision making, and *justified agency*, which explains choices in terms of social norms. Along the way, I also propose some hypotheses about self explanation that merit further study.

ASPECTS OF EXPLANATION

Two aspects of human explanations place constraints on AI approaches to replicating their generation. First, they invariably involve some form of *cognitive structure* that relates items of interest. For instance, a diagnosis links observed symptoms to hypothesized problems, often through multiple steps. Second, these structures typically comprise elements of *knowledge* that have been instantiated for the task at hand. Thus, the steps in a diagnosis might be instances of generic rules that relate symptoms to causes. Explanatory structures vary along a number of dimensions. They may be entirely qualitative, as in a geometry proof, or they may include quantitative annotations, as in the solution to a physics word problem. Accounts also differ in their complexity (e.g., the number of knowledge elements) and their depth (e.g., the length of reasoning chains). Nevertheless, they share many features that one can discuss in general terms.

We should distinguish between two uses of 'explanation' that commonly appear in English. The word sometimes refers to a mental, written, or spoken *structure* that serves to elucidate some phenomena or behaviors. Thus, we refer to a scientific explanation of pulsar cycles, a mechanical explanation of how a toilet flushes, or an introspective explanation for one's home-buying decision. In other cases, the term denotes the *process* or *activity* of generating such an explanatory structure. We say that an astrophysicist engages in explanation of pulsar behavior, a plumber focuses on explanation of a leak, or a home buyer carries out explanation of his residential choice. This chapter will use both senses of the term, but its meaning should be clear from the context in which it appears.

We can further differentiate between two specializations of explanatory processes. The first refers to the *construction* of accounts for observed situations or events. A geologist posits a set of processes for the origin of a landform, a reader infers the goals of a novel's character, and a home buyer records the reasons for his decisions. The result is a cognitive structure in the explainer's own mind. The second meaning instead deals with the *communication* of such mental structures once they exist. The geologist presents a talk about his account of a landform's evolution, the reader shares with a friend his guesses about the character's motivations, and the home buyer tells his partner why he favors one house over others. This second sense applies not only to sharing accounts of external events, but also to communicating why one made a given decision or generated a particular plan. Thus, it includes the process of *self explanation*, the important specialization on which I will concentrate here.

REPRESENTING EXPLANATIONS

We have seen that explanations are cognitive structures an intelligent system can construct or communicate, so both their form and content merit discussion. Such accounts link a set of observations or decisions to each other through a set of relations that serve as connective tissue. Explanations invariably draw on background knowledge, typically at the domain level (e.g., how refrigerators operate, regulations about driving), but they sometimes involve the meta level (e.g., conventions of dialogue). However, they do not incorporate generalized knowledge elements themselves, but rather refer to *instances* of such knowledge elements that connect facts or queries to each other.

In rule-based frameworks, explanations are organized as one or more proof trees with shared subproofs, where each rule instance links observed or inferred beliefs (e.g., Ng & Mooney 1990). For instance, an account for why an automobile does not start might connect observed behaviors through instantiated rules that describe a generic car's operation (e.g., Reiter 1987). In script and frame paradigms, the knowledge elements are large enough that some accounts involve a single instantiated structure, although they can combine more than one (e.g., Shrager 1987). An explanation can also involve an analogy, where knowledge corresponds to stored cases (linked facts), one of which maps onto elements of the new situation. Any formalism (e.g., rules, scripts, frames, or cases) that encodes knowledge structures can serve in this capacity.

In addition, explanations can differ in the ontological character of the knowledge elements on which they draw. These may denote logical relations, like those in geometry proofs, but they may also incorporate numeric calculations, as arise in solutions to textbook physics problems (e.g., VanLehn & Jones 1993). Moreover, the knowledge elements can include likelihood information, as in the rules of a probabilistic context-free grammar. In such frameworks, explanations can have the same organization as in logical ones (e.g., proof trees), but they attach probabilities to constituents. Knowledge structures may also have a causal interpretation, which can be either deterministic (e.g., a broken wire leads a starter to fail) or stochastic (e.g., a loose wire sometimes causes failure). Accounts that focus on an agent's behavior may be teleological in that they refer to the goals that guide its decisions and actions (e.g., Meadows, Langley, & Emery 2014). Other explanations involve predictable patterns that lack further justification; many social norms and conventions (e.g., expected behavior in churches or restaurants) take this form.

Finally, facts can play two distinct roles in explanatory structures, as Langley and Meadows (2019) have noted. In *derivational* explanations, observations serve as root nodes in a set of connected proof trees, while rule instances or other instantiated knowledge structures show how they follow from other facts and assumptions. Many scientific explanations adopt this scheme, as do causal diagnoses and teleological plans. In *associative* explanations, observed beliefs appear only as terminal nodes, which let one deduce new beliefs that follow from these facts. Such accounts use instantiated knowledge structures to connect observations to each other, but not to derive them. Parse trees for sentences are classic instances of this paradigm, but script-based interpretations of stories also illustrate the idea. This distinction is less relevant to self explanations, our focus here, as agents have access to their reasoning chains, but some (e.g., plans) have a hierarchical or derivational structure, whereas others (e.g., schedules) are relational but nonhierarchical.

VARIETIES OF SELF EXPLANATION

With these points in mind, we can now examine three forms of self explanation[2] and how they differ. Efforts to develop new AI functionality often start with a cognitive task analysis that identifies component abilities. Elsewhere (Langley 2019) I have proposed four such abilities that underlie explainable agency:

- *Generating decision-making content.* When carrying out problem solving, the agent must consider different candidate solutions, evaluate them, and select which ones to pursue.
- *Indexing generated content.* When making decisions, the agent must store and index details about its choices in an episodic memory or similar repository.
- *Retrieving stored content.* After it has solved a problem, the agent must transform questions into cues that let it retrieve relevant information from this memory.
- *Transmitting retrieved content.* Once it has retrieved this information, the agent must translate the results into an understandable form and convey it to others.

All approaches to explainable agency must draw on their generated content, which in turn influences their downstream processing. Thus, it makes sense to discuss in some detail not the mechanisms involved in the first stage of processing, but instead the results they produce.

Structural Explanations

One form of self explanation – *structural* – clarifies how a collection of steps is *rational* in Newell's (1982) sense that an agent believes they could help achieve its goals. For instance, a plan incorporates a sequence of actions that, if carried out, should produce an end state that satisfies some goal description while not violating any known constraints. Thus, a route for driving must include contiguous segments from the starting point to the target destination. The explanatory structure shows how the steps link the goals or query to the initial situation through knowledge: it focuses on the *means* of achieving objectives. We can specify the generic task of explaining the qualitative structure of a problem solution in terms of inputs and outputs:

- *Given*: A solution to a problem that specifies steps linking the initial state to the goal description;
- *Given*: Domain knowledge that defines the problem space in which the agent sought solutions;
- *Given*: A query about whether or why the candidate is acceptable or about the role played by given steps;
- *Produce*: An explanation for why the candidate is or is not acceptable or how given steps aid the solution.

Structural explanations need not focus on successful solutions; they can also clarify why a candidate does not resolve the problem. Note that this formulation does not mention how the agent generated its reasoning chain and concerns only its logical or causal structure.

However, the details of a structural explanation can depend on the problem-solving strategy that generates it. For example, many planners find a sequence of actions that transform the initial state into one that satisfies the goal description, with each step moving closer to the objective. Other systems create partial-order plans that specify which actions must occur before others and which do not, giving a finer-grained analysis of causal dependencies. Deductive proofs specify how a conclusion follows logically from a set of given facts through chains of inference steps. Each explanation type describes structural dependences among their elements and each has a recursive character in which sub-graphs are themselves explanations. Storage happens during construction, with the causal or logical links serving as building blocks.

The character of structural explanations has implications for later stages of processing. This lets the agent answer questions like *Why did you take action A?*, *How did you achieve goal G?*, and *Why did you do A before B?*, but requires appropriate indexing, retrieval, and transmission.[3] For instance, given a partial order plan, one might index actions by the goals or subgoals they achieve and by their matched conditions. When asked a question about the role an action plays in a given plan, the agent translates the query into a retrieval cue, maps it to an appropriate index, and returns the retrieved structure. Finally, the transmission process converts this content into natural language, a diagram, or other format to provide an answer. This may invoke templates associated with different question types and instantiate them as needed, producing a response like *I turned left from Main onto Campus so I would be heading north on Campus.*

The AI literature includes some relevant research on these topics. For instance, work on analogical planning (e.g., Jones & Langley 2005; Veloso et al. 1995) has addressed generation, storage, and retrieval, but not their use for self explanation. Some expert systems recorded their reasoning and played them back on request (Clancey 1983; Swartout et al. 1991), while Johnson (1994) and van Lent et al. (2004) developed agents that recorded their decisions during execution of military missions and later answered questions about their reasoning, including what they would have done in counterfactual scenarios. In other work, Bench-Capon and Dunne (2007) adapted computational models of argument to explain how alternative conclusions are supported or contradicted by available evidence, whereas Briggs and Scheutz (2015) reported an interactive robot that gives five types of reasons why it cannot carry out a task.

Preference Explanations

A second form of self explanation focuses on the *desirability* of solutions that an agent's finds, without concern for their internal structures. This is especially relevant for tasks like route finding and job scheduling that have many possible solutions, some of which are more desirable than others. We can state the task of explaining such preferences more precisely in terms of the inputs required and the outputs produced:

- *Given*: A set of solutions that the agent has generated for some decision-making task;
- *Given*: Domain knowledge that defines a problem space of candidate solutions and their quality;
- *Given*: A query about why the agent ranks a given solution above other candidates;
- *Produce*: An explanation for why the agent prefers that solution over alternatives.

This activity is quite different from explaining how the component steps of a plan or derivation achieve some goal. Rather, it more closely resembles the task addressed by recommender systems, which often produce a ranked list of candidates for users to consider.

The distinction between structural and preference explanations is not a matter of granularity, but whether one cares about *means* of reaching results or about their overall *quality*. To clarify this point, consider a travel planner that finds multiple routes for reaching some target location. A structural account would store, for each route, the road segments and turns that lead from the start to end point, including how each step enables the next one. In contrast, a preference explanation would describe each candidate route in terms of driving distance, number of traffic lights, or other global characteristics. When multiple criteria come into play, preference accounts clarify their relative importance and how decisions resolve trade-offs. They may also specify why a candidate's score did not exceed an acceptability threshold.

The details of this self-explanation ability will depend on how the agent's scoring and ranking process operates. One common method uses a linear utility function that computes each candidate's score on k features, multiplies each score by a weight, and calculates a weighted sum, then orders candidates by this total. A second scheme uses a lexicographic function, which orders attributes by importance. Candidates are partitioned based on scores for the initial attribute, then ranked within these sets based on the second attribute, and so forth, much as words in a dictionary. A third alternative relies on preference rules that rank some candidates as better than others, without assigning numeric scores, to give a partial ordering over them.

Preference explanations support different types of questions than structural accounts. These include queries like *Why did you prefer solution X to solution Y?*, *How did X compare to Y on criterion C?*, and *Why did X not appear in the solution set?* In this case, indexing and retrieval are simple processes, as the agent can store values for individual attributes with each solution and retrieve them as needed. As before, the final transmission stage can draw on templates that specify forms of answers for alternative types of queries, although these will differ from those for structural explanations. They will also depend on whether orderings are based on a numeric evaluation function, a lexicographic scheme, or preference rules. For instance, to clarify why it favored one solution over another, the agent might unpack calculations for the two candidates, note that they tied on the first attribute but that one did better on the second, or report the rule responsible for the decision.

This emphasis on preferences does not imply that explanation must deal only with complete solution structures. For example, if a planner uses a hierarchical task network to guide its search, then a user should be able to question why it selected one subplan for a given subtask rather than an alternative. The same idea applies to a system that finds proofs using monotonic inference rules, where a user may ask why it favored one subproof over a different candidate that leads to the same intermediate conclusion. The ability to focus attention on elements of hierarchical solutions does not necessarily mean that explanations must touch on their logical structure or how they were found. Moreover, the same mechanisms for indexing, retrieving, and transmitting results can apply to any level of hierarchical explanations.

As noted above, recommender systems often rely on a learned user profile to rank candidate items like books or movies, but one can also use such profiles as heuristics to guide search on complex reasoning tasks and to rank the solutions. Rogers et al. (1999) applied this idea to route planning, drawing on a user profile, represented as weights on complete route features, to find personalized directions in a digital road map. Gervasio et al. (1999) adopted a similar approach to personalized scheduling, invoking a user profile, encoded as weights on global schedule features, to evaluate candidates and rank solutions. These two efforts are interesting because one used best-first search through a space of partial routes, whereas the other used repair-space search through a space of complete schedules. This shows that radically different search methods can produce the same type of preference accounts.

Process Explanations

The final form of self explanation focuses on the *processes* by which an agent generates its plans or other mental structures. This view revolves around the widespread assumption, which had its origins in the earliest days of artificial intelligence, that complex cognition requires heuristic search through a problem space (Newell & Simon 1976). This posits that the recipients of explanations are interested in details about how the system carried out that search, including which alternatives it considered, why it decided to pursue some in favor of others, and even when it decided to change its mind (e.g., by choosing to backtrack).

We can specify the generic task of explaining the problem-solving processes that an agent used to make its decisions and generate it solutions as:

- *Given*: An annotated search tree that stores options considered and decisions made in problem solving;
- *Given*: Domain knowledge that defines a problem space in which the agent seeks solutions;
- *Given*: A query about why the agent considered an alternative or made a choice during problem solving;
- *Produce*: An explanation for why the agent considered that alternative or made that choice.

This task formulation is similar in spirit to the generation of think-aloud protocols (Newell & Simon 1972), which gave early insights about human problem solving and which led directly to the creation of early AI systems. In this setting, a researcher presents a subject with some problem (e.g., a theorem to prove or a puzzle to solve), asking the subject to talk aloud as he works on it. The scientist records this verbal report, transcribes it, and analyzes it to understand the subject's thinking processes. One important difference is that our explanation task occurs after problem solving is complete.

As before, the details of process explanations differ considerably depending on the problem-solving strategy. For instance, a forward-chaining planner would store actions it considers at each state, including the successor states that would result and the order in which each was generated. The system would also retain its reasons for pursuing one option before others, as well as reasons for backtracking or declaring success. In contrast, a means-ends problem solver would record its reasons for selecting a goal on which to focus or an action on which to chain backward. Alternatively, a case-based planner would note why it favored one retrieved solution over competitors, why it took certain adaptation steps, and so forth. Even within the same framework and given the same goals, different heuristics can guide search down different paths. This means that different problem solvers can arrive at the same solutions by divergent trajectories, each of which constitutes a separate process account of the agent's decision making.

Process explanations combine elements of structural and preference accounts, the key difference being that they retain decisions about the search effort itself rather than only about solutions. As a result, they support questions like *Why did you select action A on step S?*, *How did you achieve goal G on step S?*, *Why did you prefer A over B on step S?*, and *Why did you backtrack after trying action A?* Note that each of these refers to some point in the search process, as the agent may consider the same action or goal in different contexts. Thus, the agent must incorporate this information during indexing and retrieval in addition to the cues used for structural and preference accounts. There appears to have been little AI research on storing, retrieving, and transmitting process explanations either during problem solving or during retrospective reports, although studies of verbal protocols (Ericsson & Simon 1984) offer clues about the mechanisms that produce them.

The concern with traces of decision making raises the question of what counts as a legitimate process explanation. People are good at generating verbal protocols during problem solving, but they are notoriously unreliable at reproducing their reasoning later and instead often provide at least partial rationalizations. Such reconstructions are similar to accounts of external events, in that they explain incomplete memories in terms of plausible inferences over background knowledge. This form of explanation is relevant to modeling humans, but it is less defensible when developing synthetic agents, which need not suffer from the same memory limitations. For most applications, researchers can assume that process accounts are based on accurate traces based on the decision maker's actual reasoning and conclusions.

Hypotheses about Explanation Types

Now that we have identified and characterized three forms of self explanations, we can ask which of them is most useful to humans who interact with intelligent agents. Some might argue that process explanations are the natural choice, as they provide more details and thus will offer greater insight into an agent's operation. Others might instead hold that structural or preference accounts are inherently superior, because people have no need to know how an intelligent system decided on its actions but will care only how it achieved the objectives how it ranked the alternative solutions.

I will not take either position, but instead claim that the most appropriate form of self explanation depends on its intended purpose.

This argument assumes that there are different types of consumers, which leads to two hypotheses. We can state the first as:

- *Process explanations will be favored by researchers interested in the details of problem solving.*

This conjecture posits that some users care primarily about the process of finding solutions. This group includes cognitive psychologists who want to understand the ways in which an intelligent system mimics, or fails to mimic, a human problem solver. Yet it also includes many AI researchers who are concerned with the detailed operation of their AI systems, both for debugging purposes and for improving the effectiveness of their search mechanisms.

However, not all people who interact with intelligent systems will care about detailed traces of their problem-solving behavior. This suggests a second conjecture, which we can state as:

- *Structural and process explanations will be favored by users interested in outcomes of problem solving.*

This group includes end users of autonomous agents who had no role in their development. These are analogous to people who use recommender systems but have little idea how they operate, but who still want to know why one option was ranked as better than another. But it will also include AI researchers, and even psychologists, who are concerned more with the correctness of solutions and the criteria used to evaluate them than with the mechanisms used to find them. Preference accounts are likely to be more useful on tasks that involve many solutions of differing quality.

NORMATIVE AGENCY

Explainable agency is linked to the pursuit of goals, but not all goals are egocentric, which requires us to take a slight detour, as humans must operate within their societies. When a hungry person seeks food, he buys it rather than stealing it. When a passenger wants to board a bus, she waits in a queue rather than cutting in front of others. When a soldier desires sleep, he nevertheless gets up when he hears reveille. In other words, people generally follow the *norms* of their society. These may involve formal laws, military orders, informal customs, or moral tenets, but they all influence and canalize behavior in certain directions, and we would like intelligent agents to behave in similar ways. We will say that:

- *An intelligent system exhibits* ***normative agency*** *if, to the extent possible, it follows its society's norms.*

Let us return to the domain of autonomous vehicles. Clearly, we want self-driving cars to obey established laws, such as staying within the posted speed limit, driving on the correct side of the road, and stopping at red lights. However, we also want them to follow informal customs, such as not cutting in front of other vehicles and moving over to let faster ones pass. At the same time, we want them to realize that norms may come into conflict and they may need to favor some at the expense of others.

Consider a scenario in which a driver takes a friend with a ruptured appendix to the hospital. He exceeds the speed limit, weaves in and out of traffic, slows for red lights but then runs them, and even drives briefly on a sidewalk, although he is still careful to avoid hitting other cars or losing control on turns. The driver takes these drastic actions because he thinks the passenger's life is in danger, so reaching medical treatment rapidly is more important than being polite to others along the way or obeying routine traffic laws. This example of normative agency illustrates that societal norms can conflict with each other and thus requires reasoning about trade-offs. The scenario also reminds us that driving is a far more complex task than simply staying on the road and avoiding collisions.

Before intelligent agents can use norms to guide behavior in such a human-like manner, we must first decide what content they will encode. One option is to specify what actions the agent should or should not carry out in certain classes of situations. This view is closely related to *deontological* accounts of ethics, championed by Kant, which emphasize fulfilling one's duties or obligations. Another choice is to associate different values with distinct states and to favor actions that produce better outcomes. This idea is linked to *consequentialist* approaches to ethics, due originally to Hume, Bentham, and Mill, with utilitarianism an important special case. At first glance, these frameworks appear to be competitors, but Spranca, Minsk, and Baron (1991) report studies that suggest people use a mixture of deontic and consequentialist methods.

A related issue concerns how an intelligent agent represents such normative content. One approach, adopted by Mikhail (2007), specifies moral tenets using logical rules, much as one can do with many formal laws. A second alternative is to state norms in terms of numeric value functions, like those used in many game-playing systems. Rules are often linked to deontic frameworks and value functions to consequentialist ones, but one can also apply rules to states and functions to actions. These approaches seem mutually exclusive, but Iba and Langley (2011) have shown how they map onto an agent architecture that associates numeric values with rule-generated structures. Norms can also specify both prescribed and proscribed actions or states (Malle et al. 2015), akin to positive and negated 'trajectory' goals.

To develop human-like normative agents, the research community must address a number of open issues that deserve attention. These include extending intelligent systems to handle:

- *Conditional values.* We can easily associate numeric values with normative rules, but some norms may only come into play in certain contexts, and their importance may vary with situational factors. Thus, we must develop representations for laws, morals, and other norms that specify conditional values or utilities.
- *Trade-offs among norms.* In some cases, norms are incompatible, forcing the agent to decide which to obey and which to ignore. We must develop agent architectures that examine the values of relevant norms, evaluate trade-offs among different choices, and select plans or actions that give better overall scores.
- *Mitigating factors.* The importance of norms can be altered by other factors that make their violation no less serious but more forgivable. We must develop representations of such mitigating factors and methods for combining them when making choices about actions.
- *Domain-independent norms.* Many norms are domain specific, but others are quite general, like being sensitive to a friend's concerns or avoiding unnecessary emotional harm. These require formalisms for beliefs about others' mental states and ways to combine such constraints with domain-level concerns.

The AI literature reports some work on such normative reasoning, with the earliest focused on legal inference (e.g., Branting 2000). Equally relevant has been research on machine ethics and moral reasoning (e.g., Anderson et al. 2006; Bringsjord et al. 2006; Dehghani et al. 2008;

Guarini 2005; McLaren 2005). Some researchers have developed new representations and mechanisms to support normative judgments and decisions, but others (Iba & Langley 2011; Liu et al. 2013) have treated moral reasoning as a form of everyday cognition. Authors have demonstrated their systems on a variety of scenarios, showing that AI can address many aspects of legal, moral, and other normative reasoning, but this remains a relatively unexplored arena.

JUSTIFIED AGENCY

Although people can explain their goal-oriented activities, many of their accounts incorporate societal norms. When a pedestrian clarifies why he followed an indirect path, he may say that he did it to avoid walking across a neighbor's lawn. When a homeless person is asked why he begs for a handout rather than mugging someone, he might state that he knew the latter was against the law. And when a shopper explains why she let another customer with only a few items check out ahead of her, she might say that, if their positions were reversed, she would have appreciated the same treatment. Our explanations often include a mixture of personal goals and more generic social constraints. We maintain that intelligent agents should demonstrate similar abilities and we will say that:

- *An intelligent system exhibits* ***justified agency*** *if it follows its society's norms to the extent possible and if it explains its activities in those terms.*

Let us return to the example of taking someone with peritonitis to the emergency room, driving aggressively and breaking traffic laws along the way. This scenario is interesting because the explanation revolves almost entirely around social norms – not only the laws and customs the driver chose to ignore, but the idea that saving someone's life should take precedence over other factors. Personal goals come into play, such as avoiding collisions and not turning over, but they also support this top-level normative aim.

If we want to develop justified agents of this sort, we must decide on how their justifications map onto the three forms of explanations discussed earlier. Recall that structural accounts specify how a sequence of steps leads to the agent's goals, so the natural response is to replace some egocentric goals with societal ones. Many societal norms specify actions or states that the agent should avoid while achieving its aims, but we can encode these in much the same way as trajectory constraints in AI planning systems. Preference explanations specify the overall qualities of problem solutions, values of their constituents, and how these are combined. They are relevant to scenarios that involve trade-offs among norms, where the agent must balance societal aims against each other or against its own. Process accounts that describe the course of the agent's decision making, including structural relations and preferences, can also incorporate social norms.

Thus, initial analysis suggests there are no serious obstacles to adapting the three types of self explanation to include norms in support of justified activities. When generating, evaluating, and storing plans, a justified agent must encode, consider, and record not only its personal goals but also social concerns. Some justifications will treat norms as hard constraints that forced the agent to carry out some actions and avoid others, but others will include reasoning about trade-offs that arose when norms came into conflict. When asked a question about its activities, the agent must be able to retrieve the ways in which its choices relate to norms and then communicate them in accessible terms. This leads to another hypothesis:

- *Any intelligent system that supports explainable agency and normative agency will exhibit justified agency.*

In other words, once we have developed the representations and mechanisms to support the first two abilities, we will need no additional structures or processes to let agents justify their activities in normative terms. If we simply augment our goals and preferences with similar encodings of social mores, then we will obtain justified agency with no extra effort. This means that developing agents with the ability to justify their behavior will not be as difficult as it first appears.

Some readers will think that this conclusion follows logically from our definitions, but it is actually a scientific hypothesis that merits empirical tests. The definition of justified agency requires that it incorporate both the ability to explain decisions and to reason about norms, but it does not imply these alone are sufficient. For example, agency may be more complex than we have posited (Bello & Bridewell 2017) and fuller analysis may reveal that norms demand richer forms of explanation. Similarly, taking such factors into account during plan generation may depend on reasoning beyond that needed with goals and utilities, or answering normative questions may require new forms of response. Such extensions may not be necessary, but we need further research to determine whether the hypothesis is accurate.

One can also ask which form of self explanation is more relevant to settings that require justified agency. We have already seen that social norms can appear, in different guises, in structural, preference, and process accounts. However, the most challenging instances of justified agency in humans involve conflicts and trade-offs among norms. These are the mainstay of moral dilemmas studied by philosophers, but they also occur in legal cases and everyday life. The centrality of trade-offs suggests that preference explanations will play the most important role in justified agency, but we must develop intelligent systems that communicate their reasoning about social norms to test this conjecture.

CONCLUDING REMARKS

In this chapter, I defined the notion of explainable agents, which convey the reasons behind their decisions and actions. I also distinguished among three varieties of self explanation – structural, preference, and process – that store different types of content and I hypothesized when each of them is likely to be most useful. In each case, I examined how these accounts might be encoded, along with their implications for indexing, retrieval, and transmission. After this, I introduced the idea of normative agents, which attempt to follow societal maxims, and justified agents, which explain their decisions and activities in terms of those norms, along with a conjecture that joining explainable and normative agency will enable justified agency with no additional effort.

The theoretical analysis that I offered for explainable, normative, and justified agency is far from complete, but it suggests clear avenues for how to elaborate it. Researchers interested in the topic should develop architectures for agents that support all three types of self explanation, develop normative agents that guide their decisions by knowledge about social norms, and combine these elements to produce justified agents. They should demonstrate and evaluate these agents' ability to plan and act in complex domains (e.g., in urban driving simulations), to take into account laws, customs, and moral tenets when making decisions in these settings, and to answer questions about the reasons for these decisions. Undoubtedly, these efforts will encounter unexpected obstacles that reveal new challenges, but they will take us closer to understanding the structures and processes needed to replicate explainable agency in humans.

ACKNOWLEDGMENTS

This chapter incorporates and elaborates on content from previous publications, including Langley et al. (2017) and Langley (2019a; 2019b; 2020). The analysis was supported by AFOSR Grant FA9550-20-1-0130 and by Grant N00014-20-1-2643 from the Office of Naval Research, neither of which are responsible for its contents. I owe thanks to many colleagues - especially David Aha, Dongkyu Choi, Ben Meadows, and Mohan Sridharan - for discussions that led to these ideas about explainable agency.

NOTES

1. This problem is arguably less challenging than postulating the reasons that another agent behaved as it did, sometimes called *plan recognition*, as the system can store and access traces of its own decision making.
2. Another important variety of self explanation addresses how the agent revised a plan during execution because unexpected events occurred.
3. In this chapter, I focus on indexing and retrieval of elements for a specified task, rather than dealing with cases in which the agent must access structures from a memory that stores results for many distinct problems.

REFERENCES

Anderson, M., Anderson, S. L., & Armen, C. (2006). An approach to computing ethics. *IEEE Intelligent Systems, 21*, 56–63.

Bello, P., & Bridewell, W. (2017). There is no agency without attention. *AI Magazine, 38*, 27–33.

Bench-Capon, T., & Dunne, P. (2007). Argumentation in artificial intelligence. *Artificial Intelligence, 171*, 619–641.

Branting, L. K. (2000). *Reasoning with rules and precedents: A computational model of legal analysis.* Dordrecht: Kluwer.

Briggs, G., & Scheutz, M. (2015). "Sorry, I can't do that:" Developing mechanisms to appropriately reject directives in human-robot interactions. In *Proceedings of the AAAI Fall Symposium on AI and HRI.* Arlington, VA: AAAI Press.

Bringsjord, S., Arkoudas, K., & Bello, P. (2006). Toward a general logicist methodology for engineering ethically correct robots. *IEEE Intelligent Systems, 21*, 38–44.

Clancey, W. J. (1983). The epistemology of a rule-based expert system: A framework for explanation. *Artificial Intelligence, 20*, 215–251.

Dehghani, M., Tomai, E., Forbus, K., & Klenk, M. (2008). An integrated reasoning approach to moral decision making. In *Proceedings of the Twenty-Third AAAI Conference on Artificial Intelligence* (pp. 1280–1286). Menlo Park, CA: AAAI Press.

Ericsson, K. A., & Simon, H. A. (1984). *Protocol analysis: Verbal reports as data.* Cambridge, MA: MIT Press.

Fox, M., Long, D., & Magazzeni, D. (2017). Explainable planning. In *Proceedings of the IJCAI-17 Workshop on Explainable AI* (pp. 24–30). Melbourne.

Gervasio, M. T., Iba, W., & Langley, P. (1999). Learning user evaluation functions for adaptive scheduling assistance. In *Proceedings of the Sixteenth International Conference on Machine Learning* (pp. 152–161). Bled, Slovenia: Morgan Kaufmann.

Guarini, M. (2005). Particularism and generalism: How AI can help us to better understand moral cognition. In *Machine Ethics: Papers from the 2005 AAAI Fall Symposium.* Menlo Park, CA: AAAI Press.

Iba, W. F., & Langley, P. (2011). Exploring moral reasoning in a cognitive architecture. In *Proceedings of the Thirty-Third Annual Meeting of the Cognitive Science Society.* Boston, MA.

Johnson, W. L. (1994). Agents that learn to explain themselves. In *Proceedings of the Twelfth National Conference on Artificial Intelligence* (pp. 1257–1263). Seattle, WA: AAAI Press.

Jones, R. M., & Langley, P. (2005). A constrained architecture for learning and problem solving. *Computational Intelligence, 21*, 480–502.

Langley, P. (2019a). Explainable, normative, and justified agency. In *Proceedings of the Thirty-Third AAAI Conference on Artificial Intelligence* (pp. 9775–9779). Honolulu, HI: AAAI Press.

Langley, P. (2019b). Varieties of explainable agency. In *Proceedings of the Second ICAPS Workshop on Explainable Planning.* Berkeley, CA.

Langley, P. (2020). Explanation in cognitive systems. *Advances in Cognitive Systems, 9*, 3–12.

Langley, P., & Meadows, B. (2019). Heuristic construction of explanations through associative abduction. *Advances in Cognitive Systems, 8*, 93–112.

Langley, P., Meadows, B., Sridharan, M., & Choi, D. (2017). Explainable agency for intelligent autonomous systems. In *Proceedings of the Twenty-Ninth Annual Conference on Innovative Applications of Artificial Intelligence* (pp. 4762–4763). San Francisco: AAAI Press.

Liu, L., Langley, P., & Meadows, B. (2013). A computational account of complex moral judgement. In *Proceedings of the Annual Meeting of the International Association for Computing and Philosophy.* College Park, MD: IACAP.

Malle, B. F., Scheutz, M., & Austerweil, J. L. (2015). Networks of social and moral norms in human and robot agents. *Proceedings of the International Conference on Robot Ethics* (pp. 3–17). Lisbon, Portugal.

McLaren, B. M. (2005). Lessons in machine ethics from the perspective of two computational models of ethical reasoning. In *Machine Ethics: Papers from the 2005 AAAI Fall Symposium.* Menlo Park, CA: AAAI Press.

Meadows, B., Langley, P., & Emery, M. (2014). An abductive approach to understanding social interactions. *Advances in Cognitive Systems, 3*, 87–106.

Mikhail, J. (2007). Universal moral grammar: Theory, evidence and the future. *Trends in Cognitive Science, 11*, 143–152.

Newell, A. (1982). The knowledge level. *Artificial Intelligence*, *18*, 87–127.

Newell, A., & Simon, H. A. (1972). *Human problem solving*. Englewood Cliffs, NJ: Prentice-Hall.

Newell, A. & Simon, H. A. (1976). Computer science as empirical inquiry: Symbols and search. *Communications of the ACM*, *19*, 113–126.

Ng, H. T. & Mooney, R. J. (1990). On the role of coherence in abductive explanation. In *Proceedings of the Eighth National Conference on Artificial Intelligence* (pp. 337–342). Cambridge, MA: AAAI Press.

Reiter, R. (1987). A theory of diagnosis from first principles. *Artificial Intelligence*, *32*, 57–95.

Rogers, S., Fiechter, C., & Langley, P. (1999). An adaptive interactive agent for route advice. In *Proceedings of the Third International Conference on Autonomous Agents* (pp. 198–205). Seattle: ACM Press.

Shrager, J. (1987). Theory change via view application in instructionless learning. *Machine Learning*, *2*, 247–276.

Smith, D. E. (2012). Planning as an iterative process. In *Proceedings of the Twenty-Sixth AAAI Conference on Artificial Intelligence* (pp. 2180–2185). Toronto: AAAI Press.

Spranca, M., Minsk, E., & Baron, J. (1991). Omission and commission in judgment and choice. *Journal of Experimental Social Psychology*, *27*, 76–105.

Swartout, W. R., & Moore, J. D. (1993). Explanation in second generation expert systems. In J.-M. David, J.-P. Krivine, & R. Simmons (Eds.), *Second Generation Expert Systems*. Berlin: Springer-Verlag.

Van Lent, M., Fisher,W., & Mancuso, M. (2004). An explainable artificial intelligence system for small-unit tactical behavior. In *Proceedings of the Nineteenth National Conference on Artificial Intelligence* (pp. 900–907). San Jose, CA: AAAI Press.

VanLehn, K., & Jones, R. M. (1993). Integration of analogical search control and explanation-based learning of correctness. In S. Minton (Ed.), *Machine Learning Methods for Planning*. San Mateo, CA: Morgan Kaufman.

Veloso, M., Carbonell, J., Perez, A., Borrajo, D., Fink, E., & Blythe, J. (1995). Integrating planning and learning: The PRODIGY architecture. *Journal of Experimental and Theoretical Artificial Intelligence*, *7*, 81–120.

Zhang, Y., Sreedharan, S., Kulkarni, A., Chakraborti, T., Zhuo, H. H., & Kambhampati, S. (2017). Plan explicability and predictability for robot task planning. In *Proceedings of the 2017 International Conference on Robotics and Automation* (pp. 1313–1320). Singapore.

CHAPTER 2

A Survey of Global Explanations in Reinforcement Learning

Yotam Amitai and Ofra Amir

Technion, Israel Institute of Technology, Haifa, Israel

INTRODUCTION

As artificial intelligence (AI) technology becomes more advanced, it is becoming increasingly integrated into society (Stone et al. 2016). From voice assistants in smartphones to online recommendation systems, AI agents are becoming a part of everyday life. In order to effectively interact with these AI agents, people need to be able to anticipate and understand their behavior. A lack of understanding of how these AI agents operate can lead to mistrust, reduced effectiveness, and even dangerous outcomes.

The idea of making AI systems explainable is itself not new. It was discussed since the early days of expert systems (Swartout 1983; Chandrasekaran et al. 1989), and more broadly relates to the literature on human-automation interaction (Janssen et al. 2019), which also considered explanations of automated systems. The maturing of AI methods and their growing complexity have led to a resurgence in interest in developing "explainable AI" methods (Aha et al. 2017; Doshi-Velez & Kim 2017; Gunning 2017).

The majority of existing explainable AI methods (often referred to as "interpretable machine learning" Doshi-Velez & Kim 2017) focus on

DOI: 10.1201/9781003355281-2

providing "local" explanations to specific decisions made by a machine learning model (e.g., showing the features that contributed most to a model's decision that a tumor is benign). Recent studies show, however, that in some cases users may be more interested in globally understanding the behavior of the model, rather than assessing it at each decision point (Jacobs et al. 2021). While some work addresses the problem of demonstrating the "global" behavior of the model, e.g., by showing examples of different tumor scans and how they were classified (Kim et al. 2016; Ribeiro et al. 2016), they still focus on one-shot decisions of classifiers and are not applicable to describing the behavior of agents acting in the world over an extended time duration. Other work explored the problem of generating plans that are more explicable to people (Cashmore et al. 2019; Chakraborti et al. 2019; Kulkarni et al. 2019), but only considered goal-based plans for short-term tasks.

The problem of explaining the behavior of reinforcement learning (RL) agents has been relatively under-studied (Alharin et al. 2020). This setting raises additional explainability challenges beyond those of explainability in supervised learning settings, as the environment is stochastic, the state space is typically large (or infinite), and the learned policy is affected by delayed rewards (i.e., an action might be taken because it benefits the agent in the long run). As in interpretable machine learning, most explainable RL (XRL) approaches focus on explaining local decisions (Anderson et al. 2020; Greydanus et al. 2017; Hayes & Shah 2017; Khan et al. 2011; Krarup et al. 2019; Madumal et al. 2020), e.g., by showing what information a game-playing agent attends to in a specific game state. However, some studies suggest that users tend to favor global explanations (Van der Waa et al. 2018) which, for supervised learning provide insights with respect to how the model classifies different instances, and in the case of RL, explain the policy or agent as opposed to a particular action.

In this chapter, we review the existing literature on *global explainable reinforcement learning* (GXRL). That is, explanations that attempt to describe to users aspects of the overall policy of an RL agent. We identify three main classes of GXRL explanations, which we categorize according to the type of explanation and describe some of the approaches in each class. We further discuss the way explanations are evaluated. We end by discussing gaps and opportunities for future work in the area.

SCOPE

In this review, we focus on global explainable RL methods for single agents (which are the focus of the vast majority of approaches). We performed a Google Scholar search on explainable reinforcement learning and reviewed the publications from several existing surveys (Cruz & Igarashi 2020; Heuillet et al. 2021; Milani et al. 2022; Puiutta & Veith 2020). We then extended the set of publications to include those that these cite as well as publications that cite them. The review is likely incomplete but covers a large fraction of the work in this area.

CHAPTER STRUCTURE

We begin with a brief background of RL and distinguish between local and global explanations of RL policies. We then classify the existing approaches into three main explanation types and describe the key approaches in each type: explanation by *representation*, explanation by *demonstration* and *rule-based* explanations. We then discuss evaluation methods and the gaps and opportunities for future work before finally concluding this chapter.

BACKGROUND: REINFORCEMENT LEARNING

Reinforcement learning (RL), as described by Sutton and Barto (2018), is a computational approach to understanding and automating goal-directed learning and sequential decision making. It distinguishes itself from other machine learning fields through its emphasis on learning from direct sequential interactions of an agent in its environment, without the need for exemplary supervision or a complete model of the environment.

The agent interacts with its environment over a series of time steps, where at each time step the agent receives an observation of the environment and takes an action based on it. The agent accumulates *rewards*, positive or negative valued, from certain states it arrives at during its sequence. The agent's goal is to maximize the cumulative reward it receives over time.

The Markov decision process (MDP) is a common mathematical framework for modeling decision-making problems where the out comes are influenced by the sequence of actions taken. It is widely used in the reinforcement learning setting. Formally, an MDP is a tuple $\langle S,\ A,\ R,\ T,\ \gamma\rangle$:

- **S:** The set of possible environment states.

- **A:** The set of possible actions available to the agent.
- **R:** A reward function $R : S \times A \rightarrow R$, mapping the transition from one state to another via an action, to a reward.
- **T:** A transition probability function $T(s, |a, s') \rightarrow [0, 1]$ $s.\ t.\ s, s' \in S, a \in A$, denoting the probability of reaching state s' by initiating action a in state s.
- γ: A discount factor, determining the importance of future rewards relative to immediate rewards.

At each time step t, the agent observes the state of the environment s_t and chooses an action a_t based on this observation. The environment then transitions to a new state s_{t+1} with probability $T(s_{t+1}|s_t, a_t)$ and the agent gains the reward $R(s_t, a_t, s_{t+1})$.

A solution to an MDP is a *policy* denoted π. An agent's policy is a probability distribution over the set of possible actions in a given state. More generally, the policy is a function, mapping a state s and action a to a probability: $\pi(s, a) \rightarrow [0, 1]$.

GLOBAL AND LOCAL EXPLANATIONS

RL explanation approaches are commonly categorized using two axes: (1) *Intrinsic vs. Post-hoc*: Frameworks dedicated to ensuring the intrinsic interpretability of the original model as opposed to post-hoc ones concerned with providing an explanation for some given (possibly black box) model in retrospect, and (2) *Local vs. Global*: Refer to the scope of what is being explained. This chapter will focus solely on the second axis, specifically, on the *global* section of its spectrum. In the context of XRL, local explanations are highly more abundant, partly due to similarities between their setup and supervised learning approaches. In this chapter we dive deep into global explanation approaches; hence, we first characterize the differences between local and global explanations.

Local explanations address the ability to understand the decisions made by a model for specific individual states. This means being able to explain what affected an agent's choice of a particular action in a given world state. Local interpretability is useful for justifying individual decisions (Doshi-Velez & Kim 2017), such as why a certain loan application was denied in the case of supervised learning, or why an action was taken by a policy in the case of RL.

Global explanations, on the other hand, refer to the ability to capture and describe general patterns and trends of a model. In the case of RL policies, this means identifying the agent's behavior, strategy, or reasoning that governs the choices it makes. In other words, global interpretability is concerned with understanding the model as a whole. Global interpretability may be useful for gaining an understanding which can be useful for debugging, detecting biases, improving the model, and ensuring that it is behaving as intended.

Both global and local interpretability are important aspects of machine learning and AI more generally. Global interpretability techniques primarily lead to establishing user trust in the model, while local ones mainly focus on inducing trust in a single prediction (Puiutta & Veith 2020).

WHAT CONSTITUTES A GLOBAL EXPLANATION?

The distinction between global and local explanations is not always clear or trivial. Indeed, when surveying previous XRL survey publications (Cruz & Igarashi 2020; Heuillet et al. 2021; Milani et al. 2022; Puiutta & Veith 2020), inconsistencies regarding this definition and the methods associated with it arose.

It can be argued that any information regarding the strategy of the agent provides some insight into its global behavior. For instance, reward decomposition methods (Juozapaitis et al. 2019) visualize the agent's expected utility for different reward components in a specific world state but also shed light on the agent's preferences more broadly. Similarly, saliency methods (Greydanus et al. 2018) visualize the focus of the agent and what it pays more attention to in a specific state and can reveal potentially generalizable insights. In this survey, we chose to focus on methods that provide global information as their main focus but discuss some aspects of local explanations in the discussion (Section 8).

Beyond the distinction between local and global explanations, the higher-level question of what constitutes an explanation is also open to debate. In this chapter, we take a broad view of explanation methods and include a variety of approaches that provide users with information regarding an agent's policy, including the use of more interpretable models (e.g., decision trees) and more descriptive approaches that demonstrate the agent's policy.

GLOBAL EXPLANATION APPROACHES

Explanation methods can be categorized through various perspectives. We chose to differentiate between methods by the explanation type, i.e. in terms of how the information is communicated to users. We attempt to answer the question "How does the described method make the element (that is being explained) more understandable?" We believe this distinction could be valuable for developing suitable benchmarks and baselines for future researchers and methods.

We identify three main explanation types:

- Interpretable representations: explanation methods that aim to make the policies of RL agents more transparent using policy representations such as decision trees.
- Demonstrations: explanation methods that aim to describe the behavior of the agent by demonstrating how the agent acts in different scenarios.
- Rule-based: explanation methods that try to present users with logical rules describing key aspects of the agent's policy.

We note that these three categories are not mutually exclusive. In particular, some of the approaches that present logical rules can also be considered interpretable representations, and any decision tree representation can be converted to a set of rules. We attempted to distinguish between interpretable representations such as decision trees that aim to present the entire policy and rule-based methods that typically show a subset of rules that may depend on a user's query.

An alternative taxonomy that was suggested in a previous XRL survey (Milani et al. 2022) is based on the RL framework element being explained; specifically, whether the explanation refers to the immediate context, denoted as feature importance (FI), the learning process and MDP (LPM), or to the policy level and behavior (PL). While this is not our main categorization, we believe it to be of complementary value for identifying gaps and trends in this area and therefore discuss it in the survey.

Methods categorized as FI primarily provide local explanations and are therefore less relevant for our survey. However, as mentioned in Section 3.1, this distinction is not always clear cut. In this survey, we have decided to include publications that explain feature importance if these were deemed to benefit or enhance global understanding. In such cases, we classified these publications either as LPM or PL.

We elaborate and provide examples for each explanation type in the following sections. We summarize the classification of the surveyed publications by explanation type and provide (1) a mapping between the categories and their explained RL element (Table 2.1), and (2) a categorization by the explanation evaluation made in each paper (Table 2.2).

TABLE 2.1 A Summary of the Classification of the Surveyed Publications Based on the Explanation Approaches and the RL Element Being Explained

Explained Element/ Explanation Type	Learning Process and MDP	Policy Level and Behavior
Interpretable Representations	Beyret et al. 2019; Shu et al. 2017	Bansal et al. 2020; Verma et al. 2018; Koul et al. 2018; Danesh et al. 2021, 69; Jhunjhunwala et al. 2020; Liu et al. 2019, 19; Bastani et al. 2018; Topin & Veloso 2019
Demonstrations	Guo et al. 2021; Dao et al. 2018; Gottesman et al. 2020	Zahavy et al. 2016; Bewley et al. 2021; Amir & Amir 2018; Sequeira & Gervasio 2020; Amitai & Amir 2023; Amitai & Amir 2022; Rupprecht et al. 2019; Huang et al. 2018; Huang et al. 2019; Lage et al. 2019; Boggess et al. 2022
Rule-based	–	Hein et al. 2017; Hein et al. 2018; Zhang et al. 2021; Hayes & Shah 2017; Sreedharan et al. 2020; Bewley et al. 2021; Landajuela et al. 2021; Finkelstein et al. 2022; Van der Waa et al. 2018

TABLE 2.2 A Summary of the Classification of the Surveyed Publications Based on the Explanation Type and Evaluation Approaches

Evaluation Approach/ Explanation Type	Computational	Case Studies	User Studies
Interpretable Representations	Liu et al. 2019; Coppens et al. 2019; Bastani et al. 2018; Topin & Veloso 2019; Verma et al. 2018; Jhunjhunwala et al. 2020; Silva et al. 2020; Topin et al 2021; Beyret et al. 2019; Shu et al. 2017	Liu et al. 2019; Coppens et al. 2019; Bastani et al. 2018, 41; Koul et al. 2018; Danesh et al. 2021	Silva et al. 2020

(Continued)

TABLE 2.2 (Continued) A Summary of the Classification of the Surveyed Publications Based on the Explanation Type and Evaluation Approaches

Evaluation Approach/ Explanation Type	Computational	Case Studies	User Studies
Demonstrations	Lage et al. 2019; Huang et al. 2019; Guo et al. 2021; Bewley et al. 2021	Gottesman et al. 2020; Dao et al. 2018; Guo et al. 2021; Rupprecht et al. 2019; Zahavy et al. 2016; Bewley et al. 2021	Boggess et al. 2022; Amitai & Amir 2022; Amitai & Amir 2023; Sequeira & Gervasio 2020; Huang et al. 2019; Amir & Amir 2018; Huang et al. 2018; Lage et al. 2019
Rule-based	Zhang et al. 2021; Landajuela et al. 2021; Hein et al. 2018; Hein et al. 2017; Sreedharan et al. 2020; Finkelstein et al. 2022	Bewley et al. 2021; Hayes & Shah 2017; Hein et al. 2018; Hein et al. 2017	Sreedharan et al. 2020; Van der Waa et al. 2018

EXPLANATION THROUGH INTERPRETABLE REPRESENTATION

One of the main approaches to GXRL aims to make the policies of RL agents more interpretable by using simpler representations of either the learned policy or of the problem structure itself (i.e., the underlying MDP).

Several methods have been proposed to approximate a DQN using some form of decision tree (Bastani et al. 2018; Coppens et al. 2019; Jhunjhunwala et al. 2020; Liu et al. 2019; Silva et al. 2020; Topin et al. 2021). For instance, Bastani et al. (2018) proposed the VIPER algorithm, which learns a decision tree policy guided by an oracle DNN policy, and showed that the decision tree achieved performance that is close to that of the DNN. Another work proposed an intrinsic explainability approach, using Iterative Bounding MDPs for which it is guaranteed that there exists a decision tree policy that can accurately capture any learned policy (Topin et al. 2021).

A different approach for elucidating agent policies is by applying abstractions. Such methods include learning a relatively small, finite representation of recurrent policy networks (Koul et al. 2018, 20) or generating abstracted policy graphs that summarize a policy (Topin & Veloso 2019).

Another form of abstraction is through generating hierarchical representations. In hierarchical reinforcement learning (Barto & Mahadevan 2003), multiple levels of abstraction are introduced, often by utilizing multiple policies that interact with one another. Each policy is either aimed at solving a unique sub-task (low-level) or dictating which policy to enact and when (high-level). These policies can be generated, for example, by decomposing the agent's task into sub-tasks (Beyret et al. 2019; Shu et al. 2017).

Verma et al. (2018) developed the PIRL framework for representing and generating policies in a human-readable form by using a domain-specific high-level programming language.

EXPLANATION BY DEMONSTRATION

Some work attempts to explain a policy to the user by demonstrating the actions taken by the policy in some example world states. These demonstrations can improve users' mental models of how the agent acts (Dragan & Srinivasa 2014).

One formulation of explanations by demonstration is "policy summarization" (Amir et al. 2018, 2019). In policy summarization, the input is the policy of an agent and a budget k for the amount of information that can be included in the summary, and the output is a summary consisting of k state-action pairs demonstrating the behavior of the agent in selected world states. Several approaches have been proposed in the literature for selecting which state-action pairs to include in the summary. Some approaches use heuristics that aim to quantify the importance or interestingness of a state (Amir & Amir 2018; Huang et al. 2018; Sequeira & Gervasio 2020). For instance, a state might be considered important if the decision taken at that state has a substantial impact on the agent's long-term utility, as quantified by the differences between the Q-values of alternative actions that can be taken in that state (Amir & Amir 2018; Huang et al. 2018). Other measures of interestingness included the likelihood of reaching a state and global minima or maxima (Sequeira & Gervasio 2020). The DISAGREEMENTS summary method aims to compare two policies by selecting states where the policies diverge (Amitai & Amir 2022)]. A different approach to policy summaries utilizes machine teaching methods and aims to optimize the summary for policy reconstruction, i.e., by selecting state-action pairs that allow recovering the original policy (Huang et al. 2019; Lage et al. 2019). Policy summarization has also been extended to summarize multi-agent policies (Boggess et al. 2022).

Other approaches do not generate a summary, but rather extract specific states based on some criteria. Guo et al. (2021) suggest a method that presents states based on their importance to the reward function. Rupprecht et al. (2019) suggest a method for generating states of interest that can be defined based on a target function (e.g., generating world states where the agent evaluates all actions highly).

Finally, Amitai et al. (2023) designed an interactive system that allows users to formulate queries about an agent's behavior (e.g., by formulating a start state and an end state) and retrieves demonstrations of the agent acting in scenarios that correspond to the given specification.

Some work presented methods for explaining the training of the agent by demonstration. For example, Gottesman et al. (2020) explain policies that were learned offline by presenting to users transitions from the training data that had a substantial influence on the learned policy. Dao et al. (2018) monitor deep RL by memorizing important moments during training and store snapshots of these moments that can be presented to users and help interpret the learned policy.

Zahavy et al. (2016) depict the relation between states through their embedding in the last hidden state of the DQN, and visualize it using a t-SNE projection and saliency to discover and identify state clusters and patterns that correlate to behavior.

RULE-BASED EXPLANATIONS

Another way to describe an agent's global behavior is by describing underlying patterns that dictate how the agent behaves in different situations. Rule extraction is the process of identifying and extracting such rules or patterns from a given data set. These rules can typically be expressed in the form of "if-then" statements, where the "if" specifies the conditions under which a particular action should be taken, and the "then" part specifies the action that should be taken. In the context of global explanations of policies, a set of logical rules describing the behavior of the agent can provide users with a global understanding of the policy. This approach shares some similarities with the approaches that use a decision tree policy in that each leaf node in the decision tree can be considered a rule. However, the approaches we review in this section differ in that the explanation to the user is given as a set of rules.

Different methods have been proposed for extracting logical rules that describe aspects of a policy. Some approaches use an underlying decision tree (similarly to those described in Section 4) and extract rules based on it (Bewley et al. 2021). Hein et al. (2017) leverage particle swarm optimization on past agent transitions to identify and generate a set of *if-then* rules (fuzzy-logic controllers). Hein et al. (2018) utilizes genetic programming to automatically extract formulas describing the agent policy from previous agent trajectories while controlling for their level of complexity. Sreedharan et al. (2020) define the concept of MDP landmarks as environment conditions, described through propositional formulas, which must be achieved in order for the agent to reach its goal. Their method, TLdR, identifies these landmarks and displays in graphical form possible routes for reaching the goal state through the transition between them. Hayes and Shah (Hayes & Shah 2017) develop an interactive approach that allows querying the agent regarding when or why an action will take place. Using statistical analysis, the states relevant to the query are identified and the minimal Boolean logic expression that covers these is obtained and converted to text. Similarly, van der Waa et al. (2018) generate textual explanations for an agent's behavior when given a contrastive query as input using a modified MDP that abstracts the state space into classes and the rewards into concepts.

Other approaches generate a symbolic policy (Landajuela et al. 2021; Zhang et al. 2021). For instance, Landajuela et al. (2021) describe a method that generates symbolic policies by modeling agent trajectories as mathematical transitions on a symbolic expression tree. Zhang et al. (2021) propose generating interpretable and verifiable logic rules by learning an unconstrained policy via an MLP-based Q-function and projecting it into a constrained policy space using symbolic compilers. Their method, deep symbolic policy, iteratively searches for mathematical expressions to be used as policies.

Finally, Finkelstein et al. (2022) explain the gap between an anticipated policy, provided by the user, and the agent's true policy, by identifying which transformations to the MDP generate an agent that acts in the anticipated way.

EVALUATION METHODS

A key challenge in explainable AI in general is evaluating the usefulness of explanations. Various metrics have been previously proposed in the literature (Hoffman et al. 2018). However, the evaluation problem is inherently context-dependent, as ultimately the question is whether the explanation was useful for downstream user tasks and this can vary depending on the user's goal, role, or expertise. The evaluation of global explanations is particularly challenging since the notion of explaining the behavior of a policy can be ambiguous.

In this section, we review and summarize the evaluation methods used in the surveyed publications. Broadly, these can be divided into three categories: (1) computational evaluation that does not involve any assessment with users and often does not include any evaluation of the usefulness of the explanation itself, (2) case studies that typically display specific examples of how the explanations might shed light on the policy, and (3) user studies that assess the effect of showing the explanation to users. We also discuss the particular tasks used in these evaluations. Table 2.2 classifies the surveyed publications based on the evaluation approach (as well as by the explanation type).

Computational Evaluations. Many of the studies on global explanations include some form of computational evaluation. These evaluations typically focus on quantitative measures related to the fidelity of the explanation, and the complexity of the explanation. Computational evaluations are particularly common in the interpretable representation and rule-based categories.

For example, many of the proposed approaches that employ a decision tree approximation of a complex policy assess the extent to which the simplified policy agrees with the original one (see Table 2.2). With respect to the complexity of the explanation, evaluations often assess aspects such as the size of the explanation (e.g., the number of nodes in a decision tree or the number of extracted rules).

Case Studies. A very common evaluation approach in the surveyed publications is describing some form of a case study. These case studies typically demonstrate the explanation for some examples and describe what can be inferred from these explanations. For example, Zhang et al. (2021) describe a case study of extracting rules for various tasks such as car avoidance and then show which rules were extracted for the learned policy. Some case studies also include more specific analyses that are facilitated based on the explanations. For instance, this may involve verifying the correctness of a policy based on a simplified representation (Bastani et al. 2018), computing feature importance (Jhunjhunwala et al. 2020), or comparing an expert description of the agent to the description based on the explanations (Hayes & Shah 2017).

User Studies. We advocate that explanations should be evaluated based on user studies and experiments that examine their effect on the intended user audience of the explanations. Conducting these studies has the potential to (1) elucidate true user needs and preferences and (2) indicate the usefulness and benefits of proposed methods to downstream user tasks. However, fewer than half of the publications we surveyed included such studies. Notably, all work in the demonstration explanation category included a case study or some form of a user study, while few of the publications in other categories described user studies that go beyond small case studies. In general, the number of participants in the user studies ranged from about 15–200 (mean of 40 participants).

Each user study included some form of task that users were asked to perform, and examined whether explanations helped users in the task, compared to some baseline explanations or no explanations. Some studies included only subjective questions. For example, one study showed examples of contrastive explanations to participants and asked them to select the explanation that most helped them understand the agent's behavior (Van der Waa et al. 2018). Additional subjective measures included the explainability assessment scale suggested by Hoffman et al. (2018).

Other studies included both subjective and objective measures. One type of objective task was determining which of two alternative agents would perform better on a task (Amir & Amir 2018; Amitai & Amir 2022). In this study, policy summaries of alternative agents were shown and users were asked which agent they would select for the task (while the agents' true capabilities, i.e. the ground truth, is known to the authors). Another objective task used for evaluation is asking users to predict what the agent would do in different scenarios (world states) (Boggess et al. 2022; Huang et al. 2019; Lage et al. 2019; Sequeira & Gervasio 2020; Silva et al. 2020). This task requires the user to generalize and infer the agent's policy based on the explanation. Additional tasks include identifying an agent's preferences (with the ground truth being based on its reward function) (Amitai et al. 2023; Sequeira & Gervasio 2020) and identifying areas in which the agent needs to improve (Sequeira & Gervasio 2020).

DISCUSSION: DIMENSIONS, GAPS, AND TRENDS

There are now many approaches that approximate a complex policy (typically, a DQN) with a simpler representation of the policy. There are also several approaches for extracting rules describing key aspects of a policy. These two classes of explanations are similar in that they aim to provide a simplified view of the policy. They differ mainly in how the explanation is represented (e.g., a complete decision tree vs. a list of rules). The third major class of explanations aims at describing a policy by demonstrating its behavior in a subset of regions in the state space. The review of the emerging literature on global explainable RL highlights the current areas of focus in the communities, as well as areas that could benefit from further exploration.

Lack of Consistent Standards. While the literature in Global XRL is growing, it lacks consistency in standards and definitions. This has also been pointed out for the XAI literature more broadly (Lipton 2018). Work in the area makes different, and often implicit, assumptions regarding what explainability for RL means. The goal of the explanation as well as the intended users of the explanations often remain unstated or vague (e.g., "improve user understanding of the policy"). Several reviews of XRL have offered dimensions along which approaches to XRL can be classified, but currently, this is done retrospectively.

Moving forward, we propose that work on this area clearly state the following:

- Explanation goal: what user tasks does the explanation aim to support? e.g., policy debugging, comparison of policies, etc.
- Intended users: who will be presented with the explanations? e.g., model developers, domain experts, or end-users.
- Explained RL Element:[1] What is being explained? e.g., are we explaining the policy, the underlying MDP, the reward function, etc.
- Explanation approach: How is the information explained? e.g., by a simplified policy representation, rules, demonstrations, etc.[1] We believe that by better specifying these aspects, it will be easier to design explanations that are useful for supporting users' tasks. Additionally, these distinctions will highlight which methods should be compared and evaluated as baselines for future work and possibly help establish benchmark standards. Importantly, better distilling the goals of the explanation methods would also guide the design of more informative evaluation methods, as discussed next.

Gaps in Evaluation. There is currently no clear standard for evaluating explainable RL methods. A large fraction of studies includes only computational evaluations. Such evaluations are important for ensuring, for example, that an approach that claims to approximate a policy indeed does so accurately. However, they do not provide evidence as to the extent to which the explanations contribute to user understanding, rather than assume implicitly that this would be the case. Some work goes beyond computational evaluations and demonstrates how explanations can be useful for some tasks, or in some domains, by giving specific examples. While this is a step forward, it still does not provide strong evidence that the intended users of the explanations would be able to reach such insights, and there is a danger that the explanations will only be useful to their developers (Miller et al. 2017).

Encouragingly, there is a growing number of researchers that do conduct user studies to evaluate explanations. It would be useful for the community to draw on methods from the human-computer interaction literature and establish standards for such user studies (see, for example, evaluation discussions by Hoffman (2013)). It could also be useful to develop a set of evaluation tasks. Several such tasks have already been introduced, e.g., action prediction, assessment of agent performance, etc. There are many considerations in designing such tasks that can affect the outcomes. For instance, while predicting the decision of a policy might seem appealing, due to the typically large (often infinite) size of the state space, it is not feasible to cover it with such questions. Then, the choice of prediction tasks can be important (e.g., randomly selecting states vs. asking about frequent states). In addition, considering a prediction in a binary manner (success/failure) does not account for the extent of the mistake. A user may predict an action that the agent's policy assigns a high or low value to, and yet these cases often receive the same "score" in a user study.

The community could benefit from creating a set of benchmarks and tasks that can be used for evaluation. An immediate extension to this survey could be to distinguish and classify these tasks to their relevant "explained RL element." We note though that ultimately, the evaluation should be based on the goals of the explanation, and evaluate the contributions of the explanations to the underlying downstream user task.

Underexplored Directions and Opportunities. The review suggests that the literature on GXRL has begun to explore several directions in depth. Here we highlight additional directions that are still underexplored.

The existing methods are for the most part developed and evaluated separately, and often provide different information to the user. It could be beneficial to design systems that present the user with a set of complementary explanations that together provide a more complete picture of an agent's policy. Moreover, it might be particularly useful to explore the integration of global and local explanations, which has not yet been explored in depth (Huber et al. 2021; Septon et al. 2022).

While the literature on explainability from the social sciences (Miller 2019) suggests that useful explanations are often contrastive and provide counterfactual information, few of the existing XRL approaches present such information. The social science literature also suggests that explanations are often given as a dialogue between an "explainer" and "explainee." This implies an interactive process in which the explainee can ask for clarifications and elaborations. Currently, few XRL methods provide interactive explanations that allow the user to iteratively explore an agent's policy. Moreover, to the best of our knowledge, prior work in the area did not attempt to design global RL explanations that are tailored to specific needs elicited from users. Such attempts have been made for supervised learning models (e.g., see Liao et al. 2020), which are more commonly used in industry. Conducting such studies for RL agents could help identify additional gaps and opportunities for improved explanation methods.

When examining the categorization of global explanations to methods that explain the learning process and MDP vs. methods that explain the behavior and policy proposed by Milani et al. (Milani et al. 2022), we can see that the vast majority of methods are categorized into the latter category (Table 2.1). Developing additional methods that explain the learning process and the MDP could help address settings in which users are non-expert in the domain and need to be familiarized not only with the policy but also with the underlying world representation. These methods might also be useful for expert users who wish to debug the training process and the world simulator, which is typically only an approximation of the real world.

The vast majority of existing approaches attempt to explain the policy of a single agent. Explaining the policies of multi-agent systems presents qualitatively new challenges to GXRL. Just as planning for multi-agent systems is not simply stitching together single-agent plans, the explanations of such policies also require more than explaining the behavior of each agent in the team separately. In particular, distributed multi-agent policies require coordination and communication mechanisms. Describing and explaining these mechanisms to users will require completely new explanation methods.

Finally, most of the current work on GXRL and XRL more broadly studies the explanation question in isolation from other aspects of human-AI collaboration. Since explanations ultimately aim to support such collaboration, it would be interesting to study explanations in conjunction with problems such as collaboration and communication in human-AI teams and assess the contribution of explanations to such teamwork more explicitly.

CONCLUSION

In this chapter, we reviewed the existing literature on global explanations for reinforcement learning. We identified emerging themes in the area and the key classes of explanation methods that have been explored so far. We suggest several avenues that the community could explore to further develop this area of research, including the integration of different explanation methods, the design of new methods that focus on under-explored questions, and better standardization of evaluation methodologies. We hope that addressing the current gaps would help advance the development of global RL explanations that support users' downstream tasks when deploying and collaborating with RL agents.

NOTE

1. Based on taxonomy proposed by Milani et al. [52].

BIBLIOGRAPHY

Aha, D., Darrell, T., Pazzani, M., Reid, D., Sammut, C., & Stone, P. (2017). IJCAI-17 Workshop on Explainable AI. *IJCAI-17 Workshop on Explainable AI.*

Alharin, A., Doan, T., & Sartipi, M. (2020). Reinforcement learning interpretation methods: A survey. *IEEE Access*, 8, 171058–171077.

Amir, D., & Amir, O. (2018). Highlights: Summarizing agent behavior to people. In *Proceedings of the 17th International Conference on Autonomous Agents and MultiAgent Systems*, 1168–1176.

Amir, O., Doshi-Velez, F., & Sarne, D. (2018). Agent strategy summarization. In *Proceedings of the 17th International Conference on Autonomous Agents and MultiAgent Systems*, 1203–1207.

Amir, O., Doshi-Velez, F., & Sarne, D. (2019). Summarizing agent strategies. *Autonomous Agents and Multi-Agent Systems*, 33, 5, 628–644.

Amitai Y., & Amir O. (2022). I Don't Think So¨: Summarizing Policy Disagreements for Agent Comparison. In *Thirty-Sixth AAAI Conference on Artificial Intelligence, AAAI 2022*, AAAI Press, 5269–5276.

Amitai, Y., Avni, G., & Amir, O. (2023). ASQ-IT: Interactive Explanations for Reinforcement-Learning Agents, *arXiv preprint arXiv:2301.09941.*

Anderson, A., Dodge, J., Sadarangani, A., Juozapaitis, Z., Newman, E., Irvine, J., Chattopadhyay, S., Olson, M., Fern, A., & Burnett, M. (2020). Mental models of mere mortals with explanations of reinforcement learning. *ACM Transactions on Interactive Intelligent Systems (TiiS),* 10, 2, 1–37.

Arzate Cruz, C., & Igarashi, T. (2020). A survey on interactive reinforcement learning: Design principles and open challenges. In *Proceedings of the 2020 ACM designing interactive systems conference,* 1195–1209. https://dl.acm.org/doi/abs/10.1145/3357236.3395525

Bansal, G., Nushi, B., Kamar, E., Horvitz, E., & Weld, D. S. (2020). Optimizing ai for teamwork. *arXiv preprint arXiv:2004.13102.*

Barto, A. G., & Mahadevan, S. (2003). Recent advances in hierarchical reinforcement learning. *Discrete Event Dynamic Systems,* 13, 1, 41–77.

Bastani, O., Pu, Y., & Solar-Lezama, A. (2018). Verifiable reinforcement learning via policy extraction. *Advances in Neural Information Processing Systems,* 31.

Bewley, T., & Lawry, J. (2021). Tripletree: A versatile interpretable representation of black box agents and their environments. *Proceedings of the AAAI Conference on Artificial Intelligence,* 35, 11415–11422.

Beyret, B., Shafti, A., & Faisal, A. A. (2019). Dot-to-dot: Explainable hierarchical reinforcement learning for robotic manipulation. *2019 IEEE/RSJ International Conference on Intelligent Robots and Systems (IROS),* 5014–5019. IEEE.

Boggess, K., Kraus, S., & Feng, L. (2022). Toward policy explanations for multi-agent reinforcement learning. *arXiv preprint arXiv:2204.12568.*

Cashmore, M., Collins, A., Krarup, B., Krivic, S., Magazzeni, D., & Smith, D. (2019). Towards explainable AI planning as a service., *arXiv preprint arXiv:1908.05059.*

Chakraborti, T., Sreedharan, S., Grover, S., & Kambhampati, S. (2019). Plan explanations as model reconciliation. *2019 14th ACM/IEEE International Conference on Human-Robot Interaction,* 258–266. IEEE.

Chandrasekaran, B., Tanner, M. C., & Josephson, J. R. (1989). Explaining control strategies in problem-solving. *IEEE Intelligent Systems,* 1, 9–15.

Coppens, Y., Efthymiadis, K., Lenaerts, T., Nowé, A., Miller, T., Weber, R., & Magazzeni, D. (2019). Distilling deep reinforcement learning policies in soft decision trees. In *Proceedings of the IJCAI 2019 workshop on explainable artificial intelligence,* 1–6.

Danesh, M. H., Koul, A., Fern, A., & Khorram, S. (2021). Reunderstanding finite-state representations of recurrent policy networks. In *International Conference on Machine Learning,* 2388–2397. PMLR.

Dao, G., Mishra, I., & Lee, M. (2018). Deep reinforcement learning monitor for snapshot recording. In *2018 17th IEEE International Conference on Machine Learning and Applications (ICMLA),* 591–598. IEEE.

Doshi-Velez, F., & Kim, B. (2017). Towards a rigorous science of interpretable machine learning. *arXiv preprint arXiv:1702.08608.*

Dragan, A., Srinivasa, S. (2014). Familiarization to robot motion. In *Proceedings of the 2014 ACM/IEEE international conference on Human- robot interaction*, 366–373.

Finkelstein, M., Liu, L., Levy Schlot, N., Kolumbus, Y., Parkes, D. C., Rosenshein, J. S., & Keren, S. (2022). Explainable reinforcement learning via model transforms. *arXiv preprint arXiv:2209.12006.*

Gottesman, O., Futoma, J., Liu, Y., Parbhoo, S., Celi, L., Brunskill, E., & Doshi-Velez, F. (2020). Interpretable off-policy evaluation in reinforcement learning by highlighting influential transitions. In *International Conference on Machine Learning*, 3658–3667. PMLR.

Greydanus, S., Koul, A., Dodge, J., & Fern, A. (2017). Visualizing and understanding atari agents. *arXiv preprint arXiv:1711.00138.*

Greydanus, S., Koul, A., Dodge, J., & Fern, A. (2018). Visualizing and understanding atari agents. In *International conference on machine learning*, 1792–1801. PMLR.

Gunning, D. (2017). Explainable artificial intelligence. *Defense Advanced Research Projects Agency (DARPA), nd Web.*

Guo, W., Wu, X., Khan, U., & Xing, X. (2021). Edge: Explaining deep reinforcement learning policies. *Advances in Neural Information Processing Systems*, 34, 12222–12236.

Hayes, B., & Shah, J. A. (2017). Improving robot controller transparency through autonomous policy explanation. In *2017 12th ACM/IEEE International Conference on Human-Robot Interaction*, 303–312. IEEE.

Hein, D., Hentschel, A., Runkler, T., & Udluft, S. (2017). Particle swarm optimization for generating interpretable fuzzy reinforcement learning policies. *Engineering Applications of Artificial Intelligence*, 65, 87–98.

Hein, D., Udluft, S., & Runkler, T. A. (2018). Interpretable policies for reinforcement learning by genetic programming. *Engineering Applications of Artificial Intelligence*, 76, 158–169.

Heuillet, A., Couthouis, F., & Díaz-Rodríguez, N. (2021). Explainability in deep reinforcement learning. *Knowledge-Based Systems*, 214, 106685. https://www.sciencedirect.com/science/article/abs/pii/S0950705120308145

Hoffman, G. (2013). Evaluating fluency in human-robot collaboration. In *International conference on human-robot interaction, workshop on human-robot collaboration*, 381, 1–8.

Hoffman, R. R., Mueller, S. T., Klein, G., & Litman, J. (2018). Metrics for explainable ai: Challenges and prospects. *arXiv preprint arXiv:1812.04608.*

Huang, S. H., Bhatia, K., Abbeel, P., & Dragan, A. D. (2018). Establishing appropriate trust via critical states. In *2018 IEEE/RSJ International Conference on Intelligent Robots and Systems*, 3929–3936. IEEE.

Huang, S. H., Held, D., Abbeel, P., & Dragan, A. D. (2019). Enabling robots to communicate their objectives. *Autonomous Robots*, 43, 2, 309–326.

Huber, T., Weitz, K., André, E., & Amir, O. (2021). Local and global explanations of agent behavior: Integrating strategy summaries with saliency maps. *Artificial Intelligence*, 301, 103571.

Jacobs, M., He, J., Pradier, M., Lam, B., Ahn, A., McCoy, T., Perlis, R., Doshi-Velez, F., & Gajos, K. (2021). Designing ai for trust in collaboration in time-constrained medical decisions: A sociotechnical lens. In *Proceeding at the Conference on Human Factors in Computing Systems*, 1, 1–14.

Janssen, C. P., Donker, S. F., Brumby, D. P., & Kun, A. L. (2019). History and future of human-automation interaction. *International Journal of Human-Computer Studies*, 131, 99–107.

Jhunjhunwala, A., Lee, J., Sedwards, S., Abdelzad, V., & Czarnecki, K. (2020). Improved policy extraction via online q-value distillation. In *2020 International Joint Conference on Neural Networks*, 1–8. IEEE.

Juozapaitis, Z., Koul, A., Fern, A., Erwig, M., & Doshi-Velez, F. (2019). Explainable reinforcement learning via reward decomposition. In *IJCAI/ECAI Workshop on explainable artificial intelligence.*

Khan, O., Poupart, P., Black, J., Sucar, L. E., Morales, E. F., & Hoey, J. (2011). Automatically generated explanations for Markov Decision Processes. *Decision Theory Models for Applications in AI: Concepts and Solutions*, 144–163.

Kim, B., Khanna, R., & Koyejo, O. O. (2016). Examples are not enough, learn to criticize criticism for interpretability. In *Advances in Neural Information Processing Systems*, 2280–2288.

Koul, A., Greydanus, S., & Fern, A. (2018). Learning finite state representations of recurrent policy networks. , *arXiv preprint arXiv:1811.12530.*

Krarup, B., Cashmore, M., Magazzeni, D., & Miller, T. (2019). Model-based contrastive explanations for explainable planning.

Kulkarni, A., Zha, Y., Chakraborti, T., Vadlamudi, S. G., Zhang, Y., & Kambhampati, S. (2019). Explicable planning as minimizing distance from expected behavior. In *Proceedings of the 18th International Conference on Autonomous Agents and MultiAgent Systems*, 2075–2077. International Foundation for Autonomous Agents and Multiagent Systems.

Lage, I., Lifschitz, D., Doshi-Velez, F., & Amir, O. (2019). Exploring computational user models for agent policy summarization. In *IJCAI: proceedings of the conference*, 28, 1401. NIH Public Access.

Landajuela, M., Petersen, B. K., Kim, S., Santi-ago, C. P., Glatt, R., Mundhenk, N., Pettit, J. F., & Faissol, D. (2021). Discovering symbolic policies with deep reinforcement learning. In *International Conference on Machine Learning*, 5979–5989. PMLR.

Liao, Q. V., Gruen, D., & Miller, S. (2020). Questioning the ai: informing design practices for explainable ai user experiences. In *Proceedings of the 2020 CHI Conference on Human Factors in Computing Systems*, 1–15.

Lipton, Z. C. (2018). The mythos of model interpretability: In machine learning, the concept of interpretability is both important and slippery. *Queue*, 16, 3, 31–57.

Liu, G., Schulte, O., Zhu, W., & Li, Q. (2019). Toward inter- pretable deep reinforcement learning with linear model u-trees. In *Joint European Conference on Machine Learning and Knowledge Discovery in Databases*, 414–429. Springer.

Madumal, P., Miller, T., Sonenberg, L., & Vetere, F. (2020). Explainable reinforcement learning through a causal lens. In *Proceedings of the AAAI Conference on Artificial Intelligence*, 34, 2493–2500.

Milani, S., Topin, N., Veloso, M., & Fang, F. (2022). A survey of explainable reinforcement learning. *arXiv preprint arXiv:2202.08434*. https://arxiv.org/abs/2202.08434

Miller, T. (2019). Explanation in artificial intelligence: Insights from the social sciences. *Artificial Intelligence*, 267, 1–38.

Miller, T., Howe, P., & Sonenberg, L. (2017). Explainable AI: Beware of inmates running the asylum or: How I learnt to stop worrying and love the social and behavioural sciences. *arXiv preprint arXiv:1712.00547*.

Puiutta, E., & Veith, E. (2020). Explainable reinforcement learning: A survey. In *International cross-domain conference for machine learning and knowledge extraction*, 77–95. Springer.

Ribeiro, M. T., Singh, S., & Guestrin, C. (2016). Why should I Trust you?: Explaining the predictions of any classifier. In *Proceedings of the ACM International Conference on Knowledge Discovery and Data Mining*, 1135–1144. ACM.

Rupprecht, C., Ibrahim, C., & Pal, C. J. (2019). Finding and visualizing weaknesses of deep reinforcement learning agents. *arXiv preprint arXiv:1904.01318*.

Septon, Y., Huber, T., André, E., & Amir, O. (2022). Integrating policy summaries with reward decomposition for explaining reinforcement learning agents. *arXiv preprint arXiv:2210.11825*.

Sequeira, P., & Gervasio, M. (2020). Interestingness elements for explainable reinforcement learning: Understanding agents' capabilities and limitations. *Artificial Intelligence*, 288, 103367.

Shu, T., Xiong, C., & Socher, R. (2017). Hierarchical and interpretable skill acquisition in multi-task reinforcement learning. *arXiv preprint arXiv:1712.07294*.

Silva, A., Gombolay, M., Killian, T., Jimenez, I., & Son, S. (2020). Optimization methods for interpretable differentiable decision trees applied to reinforcement learning. In *International conference on artificial intelligence and statistics*, 1855–1865. PMLR.

Sreedharan, S., Srivastava, S., & Kambhampati, S. (2020). Tldr: Policy summarization for factored SSP problems using temporal abstractions. In *Proceedings of the International Conference on Automated Planning and Scheduling*, 30, 272–280.

Stone, P., Brooks, R., Brynjolfsson, E., Calo, R., Etzioni, O., Hager, G., Hirschberg, J., Kalyanakrishnan, S., Kamar, E., Kraus, S., Leyton-Brown, K., Parkes, D., William, P., AnnaLee, S., Julie, S., Milind, T., & Astro, T. (2016). Artificial intelligence and life in 2030. *One Hundred Year Study on Artificial Intelligence: Report of the 2015–2016 Study Panel.*

Sutton, R. S., & Barto, A. G. (2018). *Reinforcement learning: An introduction*, MIT press.

Swartout, W. R. (1983). Xplain: A system for creating and explaining expert consulting programs. *Artificial Intelligence*, 21, 3, 285–325.

Topin, N., & Veloso, M. (2019). Generation of policy-level explanations for reinforcement learning. In *Proceedings of the AAAI Conference on Artificial Intelligence*, volume 33, 2514–2521.

Topin, N., Milani, S., Fang, F., & Veloso, M. (2021). Iterative bounding MDPs: Learning interpretable policies via non-interpretable methods. In *Proceedings of the AAAI Conference on Artificial Intelligence*, volume 35, 9923–9931.

Verma, A., Murali, V., Singh, R., Kohli, P., & Chaudhuri, S. (2018). Programmatically interpretable reinforcement learning. In *International Conference on Machine Learning*, 5045–5054. PMLR.

Waa, J. V. D., Diggelen, J. V., Bosch, K. V. D., & Neerincx, M. (2018). Contrastive explanations for reinforcement learning in terms of expected consequences. *arXiv preprint arXiv:1807.08706*.

Zahavy, T., Ben-Zrihem, N., & Mannor, S. (2016). Graying the black box: Understanding DQNs. In *International conference on machine learning*, 1899–1908. PMLR.

Zhang, L., Li, X., Wang, M., & Tian, A. (2021). Off-policy differentiable logic reinforcement learning. In *Joint European Conference on Machine Learning and Knowledge Discovery in Databases*, 617–632. Springer.

CHAPTER 3

Integrated Knowledge-Based Reasoning and Data-Driven Learning for Explainable Agency in Robotics

Mohan Sridharan

Intelligent Robotics Lab, School of Computer Science, University of Birmingham, Birmingham, UK

MOTIVATION

Consider an assistive robot that has to: (a) estimate the occlusion of objects and stability of object configurations in specific scenes—Figure 3.1; and (b) compute and execute plans to achieve desired configurations. To perform these tasks, the robot extracts information from on-board sensors (e.g., camera), and reasons with this information and prior domain knowledge. The uncertainty in its perception and actuation is represented probabilistically (e.g., "I am 90% certain I saw the robotics book in the study"). The robot's prior knowledge includes knowledge of some domain attributes (e.g., the arrangement of rooms); some object attributes (e.g., shape, surface); grounding of some prepositional words (e.g., above, in) that represent the spatial relations between objects; some axioms governing actions and change in the domain (e.g., "picking up an object will cause it to be in the robot's hand"); and default statements (e.g., "books are usually

DOI: 10.1201/9781003355281-3

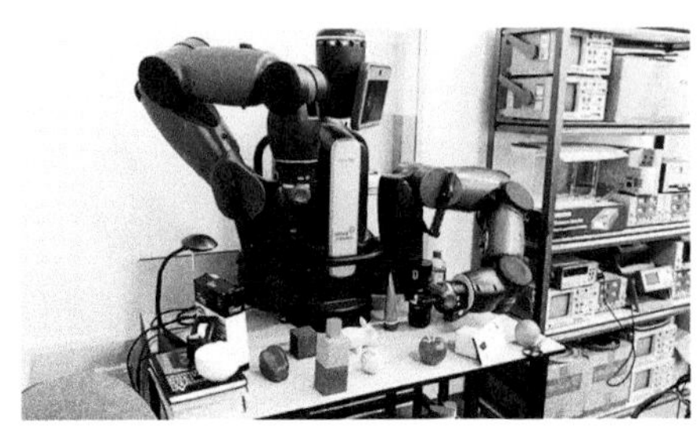

FIGURE 3.1 Scenario for some robot experiments.

in the study") that hold in all but a few exceptional circumstances (e.g., "cookbooks are in the kitchen"). Furthermore, the existing knowledge has to be revised over time, and the robot has to answer questions about its decisions and beliefs during or after planning and execution. For example, if the goal in Figure 3.1 (right) is to have the yellow ball on the orange block, and the plan is to move the blue block to the table before placing the ball on the orange block, the robot may be asked "Why do you want to pick up the blue block first?", "Why did you not pick up the pig?", or "What will happen if you rolled the ball?".

Our architecture seeks to jointly address the knowledge representation, reasoning, learning, and control challenges posed by the motivating scenario. In this chapter, we focus on the ability to provide on-demand explanations of decisions and beliefs in the form of relational descriptions of relevant objects, object attributes, actions, and robot attributes. Providing such explanations can help improve the algorithms and establish accountability, but it is difficult to do so in integrated robot systems that use knowledge-based reasoning methods (e.g., for planning) and data-driven learning methods (e.g., for object recognition). It requires the associated architecture to support the key functional capabilities of explainable agency, namely: provide on-demand justification of decisions made during (or after) plan generation and execution by considering alternative choices; present information at a suitable level of abstraction; and communicate information such that it makes contact with human concepts such as beliefs and goals (Langley et al. 2017). Our architecture draws on cognitive systems research, which highlights the benefits of coupling different representations, reasoning schemes, and learning methods (Laird 2012; Winston & Holmes 2018), to implement these functional capabilities. Specifically, our architecture:

- Combines the principles of non-monotonic logical reasoning and deep learning for decision making, and automatically learns previously unknown axioms of state constraints, action preconditions, and action effects;
- Leverages the interplay between representation, reasoning, and learning to embed the principles of explainable agency, enabling a robot to provide on-demand relational descriptions of its decisions and beliefs.

These capabilities are evaluated in the context of a robot arranging objects in desired configurations, and estimating occlusion of objects and stability of object configurations, in simulated scenes and in the real world. Results indicate the ability to: (i) incrementally learn previously unknown axioms governing domain dynamics and (ii) construct explanations reliably and efficiently by automatically identifying and reasoning with the relevant knowledge. We begin with a discussion of related work (Section 2), followed by a description of the architecture (Section 3), experimental results (Section 4), and conclusions (Section 5).

RELATED WORK

Early work on explanation generation drew on research in cognition, psychology, and linguistics to characterize explanations in terms of generality, objectivity, connectivity, relevance, and information content (Friedman 1974). Subsequent studies involving human subjects have also indicated that the important attributes of good explanations include coherence, simplicity, generality, soundness, and completeness (Read & Marcus-Newhall 1993). In parallel, fundamental computational methods were developed for explaining unexpected outcomes by reasoning logically about potential causes (de Kleer & Williams 1987).

In recent years, the increasing use of AI methods in different domains has renewed the interest in understanding the decisions of these methods, with many dedicated workshops and special tracks at premier conferences. This understanding can be used to improve the underlying algorithms, and to make automated decision making more acceptable or trustworthy to humans (Anjomshoae et al. 2019; Miller 2019). Existing work in explainable AI can be broadly grouped into two categories (Sreedharan, Kulkarni, & Kambhampati 2022a). Methods in one category modify or map learned models or reasoning systems to make their decisions more interpretable, e.g., by tracing decisions back to input data (Koh & Liang 2017) or explaining the predictions of any classifier by learning equivalent interpretable models (Ribeiro, Singh, & Guestrin 2016), or biasing a planning system towards making decisions easier for humans to understand (Chakraborti, Sreedharan, & Kambhampati 2018). The other category of methods provides descriptions that make a reasoning system's decisions more transparent, e.g., explaining planning decisions (Borgo, Cashmore, & Magazzeni 2018), providing causal and temporal relations (Seegebarth et al. 2012), or reconciling the differences between the planner's decisions and the human expectations (Sreedharan, Kulkarni, & Kambhampati 2022b). Much of this research is agnostic to how an explanation is structured or assumes comprehensive domain knowledge.

Since deep networks represent the state of the art for different robotics/AI problems, methods have been developed specifically to understand the operation of these networks, e.g., by computing a heatmap of features most relevant to a deep network's outputs (Assaf & Schumann 2019). There has also been work on reasoning with learned symbolic structure, or with a learned graph encoding scene structure, in conjunction with deep networks to answer questions about images of scenes (Norcliffe-Brown, Vafeais, & Parisot 2018; Yi et al. 2018). However, these approaches do not fully integrate reasoning and learning to inform and guide each other; or use the rich commonsense domain knowledge for reliable and efficient reasoning, learning, and the generation of explanations.

This chapter focuses on integrated robot systems that combine knowledge-based and data-driven methods to reason with and learn from incomplete commonsense domain knowledge and observations. We describe an architecture that enables such a robot to generate relational descriptions of its decisions and beliefs in response to different kinds of questions. This architecture builds on our previous refinement-based architecture that represents and reasons at two coupled resolutions (Sridharan et al. 2019). It implements a theory of explanations (Sridharan & Meadows 2019), and leverages the interplay between knowledge-based reasoning and data-driven learning (Sridharan & Mota 2023) to enable the functional capabilities of explainable agency (Langley et al. 2017).

ARCHITECTURE DESCRIPTION

Our architecture encodes the principle of *step-wise iterative refinement*. It is based on tightly coupled transition diagrams at different resolutions.

These transition diagrams are described using an *action language* AL_d (Gelfond & Inclezan 2013), which has a sorted signature with statics, fluents, and actions, and supports causal laws, state constraints, and executability conditions; the fluents can be non-Boolean and axioms can be non-deterministic. The architecture may be viewed as a logician, statistician, and an explorer working together, as shown in Figure 3.2. For ease of understanding, we will limit our discussion of the architecture to two resolutions. For any given goal, the logician performs non-monotonic logical reasoning at the coarse resolution based on commonsense domain knowledge to provide a sequence of abstract actions. Each abstract transition is implemented by the statistician as a sequence of finer-granularity actions, incorporating probabilistic models of uncertainty (e.g., in perception) and communicating the outcomes to the logician. In addition, the explorer revises the existing knowledge (e.g., of action capabilities) when needed (e.g., in response to unexpected action outcomes). The interplay between the architecture's components enables the desired functional capabilities of explainable agency, with the robot providing relational descriptions of its decisions and beliefs at the desired resolution in response to queries from a human. We will use the following example to describe the architecture's components.

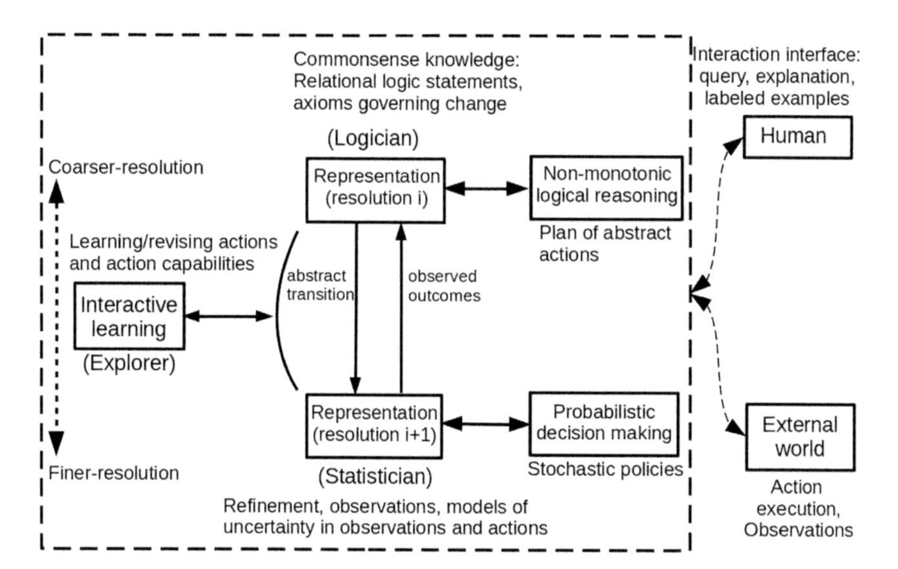

FIGURE 3.2 Our architecture leverages strengths of declarative programming, probabilistic reasoning, and interactive learning to represent, reason, and learn at different resolutions.

Example: Assistive Robotics (AR) Domain. A robot: (i) estimates occlusion of scene objects and stability of object structures, and computes and executes plans to achieve desired object configurations; and (ii) provides on-demand relational descriptions of decisions and evolution of beliefs. There is uncertainty in the robot's perception and actuation; probabilistic algorithms are used for visual object recognition and to move objects. The robot has some prior domain knowledge, which includes object attributes such as *shape* and *surface*; spatial relations between objects (e.g., above, below, behind, in); some domain attributes; and some axioms governing domain dynamics such as:

- Placing an object on top of an object with an irregular surface results in an unstable object configuration.
- Removing all objects blocking the view of an object's frontal face causes this object to be not occluded.
- An object below another object cannot be picked up.

This knowledge may need to be revised over time; some axioms and the value of some attributes may be unknown or may change, as described in Section 3.2.

Knowledge Representation and Reasoning

The coarse resolution domain description comprises system description D_c of transition diagram τ_c, a collection of AL_d statements, and history H_c. Subscript "c" refers to the coarse resolution. D_c comprises sorted signature Σ_c and axioms. For the AR domain, Σ_c includes basic sorts such as *place, thing, robot, person, object, cup, surface, and step*; statics such as *next_to(place, place)* and *obj_surface(obj, surface)*; fluents such as *loc(thing, place)*, *obj_rel(relation, object, object)*, and *in_-hand(entity, object)*; and actions such as *move(robot, place)* and *give (robot, object, person)*. Axioms in D_c (for the AR domain) are statements such as:

move(rob_1, P) **causes** loc(rob_1, P)
putdown(rob_1, Ob_1, Ob_2) **causes** obj_rel(on, Ob_1, Ob_2)
loc(O, P) **if** loc(rob_1, P), in_hand(rob_1, O)
impossible give(rob_1, O, P) **if** loc(rob_1, L_1)!= loc(P, L_2)

which correspond to two causal laws, a state constraint, and an executability condition, respectively. We also include axioms in D_c to encode theories of intention and affordance. The history H_c of a dynamic domain is typically a record of fluents observed to be true or false at a particular time step, *obs(fluent, boolean, step)*; and of actions that "happened," i.e., were executed at a particular time step, *hpd(action, step)*. This definition is expanded to represent prioritized defaults describing the values of fluents in the initial state, e.g., "books are usually in the library; if not there, they are in the office," along with exceptions (if any).

To reason with domain knowledge, we construct a program $\Pi(D_c, H_c)$ in CR-Prolog, a variant of Answer Set Prolog (ASP) that incorporates consistency restoring (CR) rules (Gebser et al. 2012). Π includes Σ_c and axioms of D_c, inertia axioms, reality checks, closed world assumptions for actions, and observations, actions, and defaults from H_c. Π also includes statements encoding information extracted from sensor inputs (e.g., spatial relations, object attributes) with sufficiently high probability. ASP is based on stable model semantics, and supports default negation, epistemic disjunction, and non-monotonic logical reasoning. Unlike "¬a" that states a is believed to be false, "not a" only implies a is not believed to be true, i.e., each literal can be true, false or unknown. An answer set of Π represents the beliefs of the robot associated with Π, with the literals at each time step representing the corresponding state. The non-monotonic logical reasoning ability enables recovery from incorrect inferences obtained due to reasoning with incomplete knowledge or noisy sensor inputs. Entailment, planning, and diagnostics can be reduced to computing answer sets of Π; we do so using the SPARC system (Balai, Gelfond, & Zhang 2013).

For any given goal, reasoning at the coarse-resolution provides a plan of abstract actions. To implement the abstract actions, we define a fine-resolution system description D_f as a refinement of D_c such that any given abstract transition between two states in τ_c has a path in τ_f between a refinement of the two states. In the AR domain, a robot would (for example) reason about grid cells in rooms and parts of objects, attributes previously abstracted away by the designer. To support interaction with the physical world, we extend D_f by introducing a theory of observation that encodes knowledge-producing actions and fluents, and non-determinism (D_{fr}). Since reasoning with D_{fr} can become computationally intractable for complex domains, we enable the robot to automatically zoom to $D_{fr}(T)$, the part of D_{fr} relevant to any given abstract transition T. Reasoning with $D_{fr}(T)$ provides a sequence of concrete actions that implement T, incorporating relevant probabilistic models of uncertainty (e.g., in perception or in the outcomes of executed actions) as appropriate. Fine-resolution outcomes with a high probability are committed to the fine-resolution history, and the corresponding coarse-resolution outcomes are added to H_c. For a more detailed description of refinement and zooming, and the use of such a knowledge representation and reasoning architecture on physical robots, please see (Sridharan et al. 2019). For an extension of this architecture to encode an adaptive theory of intentions in the coarse resolution, please see Gomez, Sridharan, & Riley (2021).

Interactive Learning

Reasoning with incomplete knowledge (e.g., to fetch target objects or estimate the occlusion of objects) can result in incorrect outcomes. The state of the art for learning previously unknown actions, axioms, or object models is based on "end-to-end" data-driven methods that require many labeled examples. It is difficult to provide such examples in complex domains or to interpret the decisions made. Figure 3.3 shows the components for learning and explanation generation in our

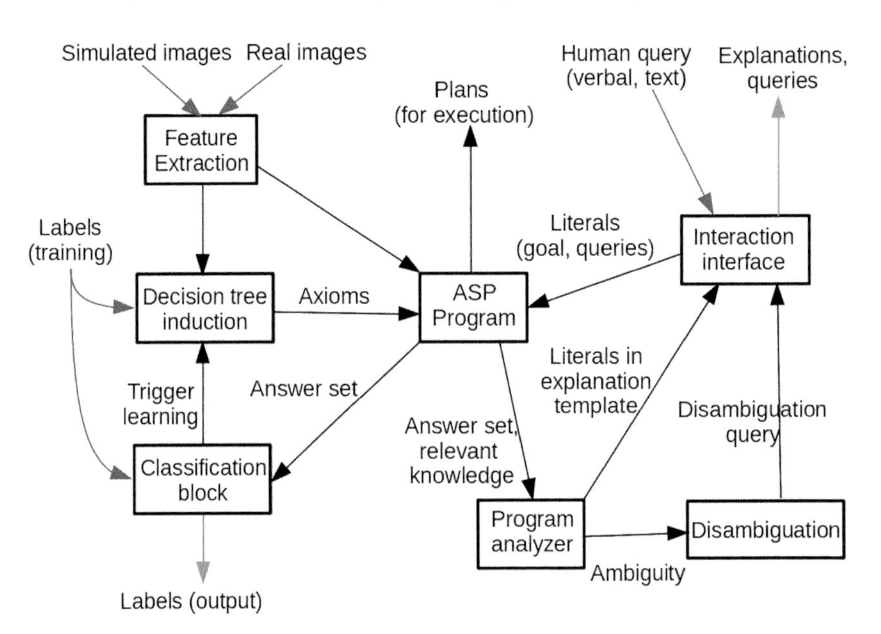

FIGURE 3.3 Non-monotonic logical reasoning guides interactive (e.g., deep, inductive) learning of previously unknown domain knowledge to complete desired estimation tasks, and to provide relational descriptions of knowledge and beliefs.

architecture, where red (green) arrows denote inputs (outputs) from (to) humans. The robot first attempts to use ASP-based logical reasoning to complete the desired tasks (e.g., planning, estimation). If this reasoning does not provide any outcome (e.g., no plan), or provides an incorrect outcome (e.g., incorrect stability label), it is considered to indicate that the knowledge is incomplete or incorrect, triggering learning. The learning component's implementation is described below in the context of the estimation tasks.

Classification Block (CNNs)

The main sensor inputs are RGB/D images that are processed to extract spatial relations and other attributes that are encoded as ASP statements. The extraction of spatial relations is based on our prior work that incrementally revises the physical world grounding of prepositional words (e.g., "in," "above") representing these relations (Mota & Sridharan 2018). For any given image, the robot tries to estimate the occlusion and stability of objects using ASP-based reasoning. If an answer is not found, or an incorrect answer is found (for training images), the robot automatically extracts relevant regions of interest (ROIs) from the image. Parameters of existing convolutional neural network (CNN) architectures (e.g., LeNet (LeCun et al. 1998), AlexNet (Krizhevsky, Sutskever, & Hinton 2012)) are tuned to map information from each ROI to the corresponding labels. The robot automatically identifies and reasons with the relevant axioms and relations to determine the ROIs; the notion of relevance is also expanded to construct explanations efficiently in Section 3.3.

Decision Tree induction

The images used to train the CNNs are considered to contain information about missing or incorrect constraints related to the estimation tasks (occlusion, stability). Image features and spatial relations extracted from ROIs in each such image, and the known occlusion and stability labels (during training), are used to incrementally learn a decision tree summarizing the corresponding state transitions. This process repeatedly splits nodes based on unused attributes likely to provide the highest entropy reduction. Trees are learned separately for different actions, and branches of a tree that satisfy minimal thresholds on purity at the leaf and on the level of support from labeled examples, are used to construct candidate constraints. Candidates without a minimal level of support on unseen examples are removed and similar axioms are merged. Specifically, axioms with the same head and some overlap in the body are grouped. Each combination of one axiom from each group is encoded in an ASP program along with axioms that are not in any group. This program is used to classify ten labeled scenes, retaining only axioms in the program that provides the highest accuracy on these scenes. Also, axioms that cease to be useful over time are removed by associating each axiom with a strength that decays exponentially if it is not used or learned again.

In addition to constraints, the robot learns previously unknown causal laws and executability conditions if there is a mismatch between the observed state after action execution and the expected state based on reasoning with existing knowledge. Any expected but unobserved fluent literal indicates missing executability condition(s); any observed unexpected fluent literal suggests missing causal law(s). Examples of learned axioms include:

$$\neg stable(A) \leftarrow obj\_relation(above, A, B), obj\_surface(B, irregular)$$
$$\neg pickup(rob_1, Ob_1) \leftarrow in\_hand(rob_1, Ob_2)$$

which correspond to a state constraint ("an object placed on another with an irregular surface is unstable") and an executability condition ("the robot cannot pick up an object if it is already holding another object"), respectively. For more details, see Sridharan & Mota (2023).

Although we do not describe it in detail in this chapter, our architecture includes a similar learning scheme for planning and diagnostics tasks. This scheme learns actions and axioms from human descriptions of desired behavior, or observations obtained through active exploration or reactive action execution in response to unexpected outcomes. Reasoning automatically limits this learning to states, actions, and observations relevant to task(s) and goal(s) at hand; see Sridharan & Meadows (2018) for more detail.

Explanation Generation

We consider an "explanation" to be a relational description of the robot's decisions or beliefs. This component is based on a theory of explanations that maps the postulates of explainable agency to: (i) claims about representing, reasoning with, and learning knowledge to support explanations; (ii) a characterization of explanations along axes based on abstraction, specificity, and verbosity; and (iii) a methodology for constructing explanations (Sridharan & Meadows 2019). This component is described below.

Interaction Interface

Human interaction with our architecture is through speech or text. Existing software and a controlled vocabulary are used to parse human verbal input and to convert text to verbal response. Specifically, human verbal input is transcribed into text from the controlled vocabulary. This (or input) text is labeled using a part-of-speech (POS) tagger, and normalized with the lemma list (Someya 1998) and related synonyms and antonyms from WordNet (Miller 1995). The processed text helps identify the type of request: a desired goal or a question about decisions, beliefs, or hypothetical situations. Any goal is sent to the ASP program for planning; the robot executes the plan, performing diagnostics and re-planning as needed, until the goal is achieved. For any question, the "Program Analyzer" considers the domain knowledge, inferred beliefs, and processed human input to automatically identify relevant axioms and literals. These literals are inserted into generic response templates based on the controlled vocabulary, resulting in (textual) descriptions that make contact with human concepts such as beliefs and goals, which are converted to synthetic speech if needed. Whenever the posed query or request is ambiguous, the robot constructs and poses queries to remove the ambiguity. Some examples of such interactions are provided in Section 4.2.

Mental Simulations

To explain the evolution of a particular belief or the (non)selection of a particular action at a particular time step, our architecture includes the ability to infer the associated sequence of beliefs and axioms. This ability is used by the "Program Analyzer" (below) to construct explanations. We adapt proof trees, which have been used to explain observations in the context of classical first-order logic statements (Ferrand, Lessaint, & Tessier 2006), to our formulation based on non-monotonic logic using the following methodology:

1. Select axioms with the target belief or action in the head.
2. Ground literals in the body of each selected axiom. Check if they are supported by the current answer set.
3. Create a new branch in a proof tree (with the target belief or action as the root) for each selected axiom supported by the answer set, and store the axiom and the related supporting ground literals in suitable nodes.

4. Repeats Steps 1–3 with the supporting ground literals in Step 3 as target beliefs in Step 1, until all branches reach a leaf node without any further supporting axioms.

Paths from the root to the leaves in these trees provide candidate explanations. If multiple paths exist, one of the shortest branches is selected and used to construct answers—see (Mota, Sridharan, & Leonardis 2021) for examples.

Program Analyzer

Algorithm 1 describes the approach for automatically identifying and reasoning with the relevant information to construct relational descriptions in response to questions or requests. It does so in the context of four types of explanatory requests or questions. The first three types were introduced in prior work as questions to be considered by any explainable planning system (Fox, Long, & Magazzeni 2017), while the fourth type considers the evolution of beliefs.

Algorithm 1: (Program Analyzer) Answer query

```
  Input: Literal of input question; Π(D, H); answer templates.
  Output: Answer and answer Literals.
  // Compute answer set
1 AS = AnswerSet(Π)
2 if question = plan description then
      // Retrieve actions from answer set
3     answer literals = Retrieve(AS, actions)
4 else if question = “why action X at step I?” then
      // Extract actions after step I
5     next actions = Retrieve(AS, actions for step > I)
      // Extract axioms influencing these actions
6     relevant axioms = Retrieve(Π, head = ¬ next actions)
      // Extract relevant literals from Answer Set
7     relevant literals = Retrieve(AS, Body(relevant axioms)
       ∈ I ∧ ∉ I + 1)
      // Output literals
8     answer literals = pair(relevant literals, next actions)
```

```
9  else if question = "why not action X at step I?" then
       // Extract axioms relevant to action
10     relevant axioms = Retrieve(Π, head = ¬ occurs(X))
       // Extract relevant literals from Answer Set
11     answer literals = Retrieve(AS, Body(relevant axioms)
        ∈ I∧ ∉ I + 1)
12 else if question = "why belief Y at step I?" then
       // Extract axioms influencing this belief
13     relevant axioms = Retrieve(Π, head = Y)
       // Extract body of axioms
14     answer literals = Recursive Examine(AS, Body(relevant axioms))
15 Construct_Answer(answer literals, answer templates)
```

1. **Plan description.** When asked to describe a particular plan, the robot parses the related answer set(s) to extract a sequence of actions of the form occurs(action1, step1), ..., occurs(actionN, stepN) (line 3, Algorithm 1). These actions are used to construct the response.

2. **Action justification: Why action X at step I?** To justify the execution of any particular action at step I:

   a. For each action A that occurred after time step I, the robot examines relevant executability condition(s) and identifies literal(s) that would prevent A's execution (lines 5–7). For the goal of placing the orange block on the table in Figure 3.1 (right), assume that the actions executed include occurs(pickup(robot, blue block), 0), occurs(putdown(robot, blue block), 1), and occurs (pickup(robot, orange block), 2). If the focus is on the first pickup action, an executability condition related to the second pickup action: ¬occurs(pickup(robot, A), I):- holds(obj_relation(below, A, B), I) is ground in the scene to obtain obj_relation(below, orange block, blue block) as a literal of interest.

   b. If any identified literal is in the answer set at the time step of interest (0 in current example), and is absent or negated in the next step, it is a reason for executing the action (X) being considered (line 7).

   c. The condition modified by the execution of the action of interest (X) is paired with the subsequent action (A) to construct the answer (line 8). For instance, the question "Why did you pick up the blue block at time step 0?", receives the answer

"I had to pick up the orange block. It was located below the blue block".

A similar approach is used to justify the selection of any particular action in a plan that has not been executed.

3. **Hypothetical actions: Why not action X at step I?** For questions about actions not selected for execution:

    a. The robot identifies executability conditions with action X in the head, i.e., conditions that (if true) would prevent X from being included in plans (line 10).

    b. For each identified executability condition, the robot examines whether literals in the body are satisfied in the corresponding answer set (line 11). If so, these literals are used to construct the answer.

    Suppose action putdown(robot, blue block, table) occurred at step 1 in Figure 3.1 (right). For the question "Why did you not put the blue block on the tennis ball at step 1?", the following executability condition is identified: ¬occurs(putdown(robot, A, B), I):- has_surface(B, irregular), which implies that an object cannot be placed on another object with an irregular surface. The answer set indicates that the tennis ball has an irregular surface. The robot answers "Because the tennis ball has an irregular surface". This process uses the mental simulations approach described above.

4. **Belief query: Why belief Y at step I?** To explain any particular belief, the robot uses the mental simulations approach to identify the supporting axioms and relevant literals to construct the answer. For example, to explain the belief that object ob_1 is unstable in step I, the robot finds the support axiom: ¬holds(stable(ob 1), I) ← holds(small_base(ob 1), I).

    Assume that the current beliefs include that ob_1 has a small base. Searching for why ob_1 is believed to have a small base identifies the axiom:

    holds(small_base(ob_1), I):- holds(relation(below, ob_2, ob_1), I),
    has_size(ob_2, small),
    has size(ob_1, big).

Asking "why do you believe object ob_1 is unstable at step I?" would yield the answer "Because object ob_2 is below object ob_1, ob_2 is small, and ob_1 is big".

Disambiguation

Questions or requests posed by humans may be ambiguous in terms of the objects or the time step that they reference. Our architecture includes a method to automatically construct questions to address such ambiguities. Inspired by findings in psychology and cognitive science (Friedman 1974; Read & Marcus-Newhall 1993), this method enables the robot to construct queries comprising the set of object attributes most likely to address the ambiguity. The method is based on three heuristic rules: (i) select attributes that match with a minimum number of ambiguous objects for the query and scene under consideration; (ii) since queries with many attributes are more likely to confuse a human, select questions with the minimum number of attributes; (iii) assign higher priority to attributes that are preferred by humans (if known) and are easy for the robot to detect. We only summarize this capability here to provide a complete description of the architecture. For more details about the heuristic rules and their use to construct disambiguation queries, see (Mota & Sridharan 2021).

EXPERIMENTAL RESULTS

We evaluated the ability of our system to learn axioms and construct relational descriptions of decisions and beliefs in response to different types of questions. Section 4.1 describes the experimental setup, followed by execution traces in Section 4.2 and quantitative results in Section 4.3.

Experimental Setup

We experimentally evaluated the following hypotheses:

H1: Our architecture supports reliable learning of unknown axioms, improving the quality of plans generated; and

H2: Leveraging the links between reasoning and learning improves the accuracy of the explanatory descriptions.

Experimental trials considered images from the robot's camera and simulated images. Real world images contained 5–7 objects of different colors, textures, shapes, and sizes in different locations of the AR domain.

The objects included cubes (blocks), a pig, a bell pepper, a tennis ball, cups, an apple, an orange, and a pot. These objects were either stacked on each other or spread on a table in different locations—see Figure 3.1 (left). A total of 40 configurations were created, each with five different goals for planning and four different questions for each plan (one for each question type), resulting in a total of 200 plans and 800 questions. We used a Baxter robot to manipulate objects on a tabletop.

Since it is difficult to explore a wide range of objects and scenes with physical robots, we also used a real-time physics engine (Bullet) to create 40 simulated images, each with 7–9 objects (3–5 stacked and the remaining on a flat surface). Objects included cylinders, spheres, cubes, a duck, and five household objects from the Yale-CMU-Berkeley dataset (apple, pitcher, mustard bottle, mug, and box of crackers). We once again considered five different goals for planning and four different questions (one for each type) for each plan, resulting in the same number of plans (200) and questions (800) as with the real-world data. To explore the interplay between reasoning and learning, we focused on the effect of learned knowledge on planning and constructing explanations. Specifically, we prepared a knowledge base in which some axioms governing the domain dynamics were missing. We then ran experiments in which our architecture learned the missing axioms over time, as described in Section 3.2, and used them for planning and explanation generation. The baseline for comparison in these experiments included the reasoning and explanation generation components of our architecture but did not support any learning (i.e., it used only the initial knowledge base with some axioms missing). During planning, the performance measures included the number of optimal, suboptimal, and incorrect plans, and the planning time. An "optimal" plan is a minimal plan; the quality of a plan was measured in terms of the ability to compute plans that require the least number of actions to achieve the goal. The quality of an explanation was measured in terms of precision and recall of the literals in the answer provided by our architecture in comparison with the expected ("ground truth") response provided manually (by the designer). Any claims of statistical significance were based on a paired t-test.

Note that the experimental setup described above does not include any studies with human subjects evaluating the quality of the explanations provided by our architecture. Such studies provide important feedback that can be used to evaluate and improve the architecture, but we leave such studies for future work. Instead, we present some execution traces describing the operation of our architecture. followed by a discussion of quantitative experimental results.

Execution Traces

The following execution traces demonstrate the capabilities of our architecture.

Execution Example 1: *[Planning and learning]*
The robot in the AR domain is in the study and it is asked to bring a cup to the study, where the goal state contains: *loc(C, study)* and *not in_hand (rob$_1$, C)*, where C is a cup.

- The computed plan of abstract actions is:

  move(rob$_1$, kitchen), pickup(rob$_1$, C), move(rob$_1$, study), putdown (rob$_1$, C)

- This plan uses the default knowledge that cups are usually in the kitchen that is next to the study.

- To implement each abstract transition T, the robot zooms to $D_f(T)$. For instance, only cells in the study and the kitchen are relevant to the first move action; irrelevant objects and locations are automatically ignored.

- The zoomed description is used to obtain a probabilistic policy that is invoked repeatedly to execute a sequence of concrete actions that implements the abstract action (e.g., robot is in a cell in the kitchen after the first move). Other actions are executed in a similar manner.

- The robot's attempt to pick up a cup in the kitchen failed. The robot observes that the cup is heavy while its arm is light. It then learns the following executability condition (written as a statement in AL_d):

  impossible pickup(rob$_1$, C) **if** arm(rob$_1$, light), obj_weight(C, heavy)

- It is also possible to learn and merge other kinds of axioms with the existing knowledge.

- The robot is also able to automatically provide on-demand explanations at a suitable level of abstraction.

Human: "Please describe the executed plan in detail."
Robot: "I moved to cell c_2 in the kitchen. I picked the large cup by its handle from the counter [...] I moved to cell c_4 of the study. I put the cup down on the red table."

Next, consider the robot's ability to provide explanations to different kinds of queries.

Execution Example 2: *[Explain plans and beliefs]*
In the scene in Figure 3.4 (left), the robot's goal is to achieve a state in which the red cube is on top of the orange cube. The following interaction takes place after the robot has executed a plan to achieve the goal.

- **Human:** "Please describe the plan."
  Baxter: "I picked up the blue cube. I put the blue cube on the table. I picked up the orange cube. I put the orange cube on the table. I picked up the red cube. I put the red cube on the orange cube."
- The robot may have to justify a particular action.
  Human: "Why did you pick up the blue cube at Step 0?"
  Baxter: "Because I had to pick up the red cube, and it was below the blue cube."
  This answer is also used to automatically highlight the relevant image regions that influenced this answer, providing additional transparency—see Figure 3.4 (left).
- The robot may have to justify the choice of actions.

FIGURE 3.4 (Left) relation between blue cube and red cube is important for the explanation in Execution Example 2; (Right) simulated image used in Execution Example 3.

Human: “Why did you not put down the orange cube on the blue cube?”
Baxter: “Because the blue cube is small.”
In the absence of any reference to a particular time step, the robot considers the single instance (in the executed plan) of putting the orange cube on another cube or surface. The answer is based on learned default knowledge that any structure with a large object on a small object is typically unstable.

- The human may ask the robot to justify beliefs.
Human: “Why did you believe that the red cube was below the blue cube in the initial state?”
Baxter: “Because I observed the red cube below the blue cube in Step 0.”

- The robot can run mental simulations to answer counterfactual (i.e., hypothetical) questions.
Human: “What will happen if the ball is rolled?”
Baxter: “The structure of blocks will be unstable.”

Execution Example 3: *[Disambiguation]*
Consider the simulated scenario in Figure 3.4 (right).

- **Human:** “Move the yellow object onto the green cube.”
There is ambiguity in the reference to a yellow object. Since the yellow cube is already on the green cube, and the yellow cylinder is below other objects, the robot poses the following clarification question.
Robot: “Should I move the yellow duck on top of the green cube?”
Human: “No. Please move the yellow cylinder on top of the green cube.”

- The robot computes the plan: *pick up the green mug; put the green mug on the table; pick up the red cube; put the red cube on the table; pick up the yellow cube; put the yellow cube on the table; pick up the yellow cylinder; put the yellow cylinder on the green cube.*

- Note that there are other equally valid plans (e.g., one that moves the yellow cube to the table first).
Human: “Why do you want to pick up the green mug?”

Robot: "I have to place the yellow cylinder on the green cube, and the yellow cylinder is below the green mug."

The robot can also trace the evolution of particular beliefs and the application of relevant axioms to answer questions after plan execution.

- **Human:** "Why did you not pick up red cube at Step 1?"
  Robot: "Because the red cube is below the green mug."
  Human: "Why did you move the yellow cube onto the table?"
  Robot: "I had to put the yellow cylinder on top of the green cube. The green cube was below the yellow cube."

Empirical Results

To evaluate **H1**, we removed five axioms (two causal laws and three executability conditions) from the robot's knowledge, and ran the learning algorithm 20 times. We measured the precision and recall of learning these axioms in each run. Table 3.1 summarizes the results. Each run was terminated if the robot executed a number of actions without detecting any inconsistency, or if the number of decision trees constructed exceeded a number. The row labeled "Strict" summarizes results when any variation in the target axiom (i.e., axioms with additional irrelevant literals) was considered to be incorrect. One example of such an axiom in which the second literal in the body is irrelevant is shown below.

¬holds(in_hand(R1, O1), I + 1):- occurs(putdown(R1, O1, O2), I), ¬holds(in_hand(R1, O5), I).

The row labeled "Relaxed" summarizes results when over-specifications were not counted as errors. High precision and recall support hypothesis **H1**.

TABLE 3.1 Precision and Recall for Learning Previously Unknown Axioms. Errors under "Strict" Mainly Correspond to the Inclusion of Additional Irrelevant Literals

Missing Axioms	Precision	Recall
Strict	69%	78%
Relaxed	96%	95%

The next set of experiments further evaluated **H1**.

1. For the 40 initial object configurations (Section 4.1), information extracted from the images corresponding to top and front views (i.e., from the camera on each gripper) was encoded as the initial state in the ASP program.
2. For each initial state, five goals were randomly encoded (one at a time) in the ASP program. The robot reasoned with the existing knowledge to create plans for these 200 combinations (40 initial states, five goals).
3. Plans were evaluated based on the number of optimal, sub-optimal, and incorrect plans, and planning time. Trials were repeated with and without the learned axioms.

Recall that our architecture reasons with a knowledge base that includes the learned axioms whereas the knowledge base used by the baseline does not include these axioms. We conducted paired trials with and without the learned axioms in the ASP program used for reasoning. The initial conditions and goal were identical in each paired trial, but differed between paired trials. We expressed the number of plans and the planning time with the learned axioms as a fraction of the corresponding values obtained by reasoning without the learned axioms. The average of these fractions over all the trials is reported in Table 3.2. We also computed the number of optimal, sub-optimal, and incorrect plans in each trial as a fraction of the total number of plans; we did this with and without the learned axioms and the average over all trials is summarized in Table 3.3.

These results indicate that for images of real scenes, reasoning with the learned axioms reduced the search space, resulting in a smaller number of plans and a reduced planning time. The use of the learned

TABLE 3.2 Number of Plans and Planning Time After Including the Learned Axioms for Reasoning (Our Architecture), Expressed as a Fraction of the Values Without Including the Learned Axioms (Baseline)

Measures	**Ratio (with/without)**	
	Real Scenes	**Simulated Scenes**
Number of steps	1.15	1.23
Number of plans	0.81	1.08
Planning time	0.96	1.02

TABLE 3.3 Number of Optimal, Sub-Optimal, and Incorrect Plans Expressed as a Fraction of the Total Number of Plans. Reasoning With the Learned Axioms (Our Architecture) Improves Performance Compared With the Baseline that Reasons Without the Learned Axioms

Plans	**Real Scenes**		**Simulated Scenes**	
	Without	**With**	**Without**	**With**
Optimal	0.4	0.9	0.14	0.3
Sub-optimal	0.11	0.1	0.46	0.7
Incorrect	0.49	0	0.4	0

axioms did not make any significant difference with the simulated scenes. This is understandable because the simulated images had more objects (than real scenes) with several of them being small objects. This increased the number of plans to achieve any given goal. Also, when the robot used the learned axioms for reasoning, it reduced the number of sub-optimal plans and eliminated all incorrect plans; almost every sub-optimal plan corresponded to a goal that could not be achieved without creating an exception to a default. Without the learned axioms, a larger fraction of the plans were sub-optimal or incorrect, particularly for simulated scenes with multiple objects. These results further support **H1**.

The next set of experiments evaluated **H2**:

1. For each of the 200 combinations from the first set of experiments with real-world data, we considered knowledge bases with and without the learned axioms and asked the robot to compute plans to achieve the goals.

2. The robot had to describe the plan and justify the choice of a particular action (chosen randomly) in the plan. Then, one parameter of the chosen action was changed randomly to ask why this new action could not be applied. Finally, a belief related to the previous two questions had to be justified—see Execution Example 2.

3. The literals present in the answers were compared against the literals in the "ground truth" response, with the average precision and recall scores shown in Table 3.4.

4. We also performed these experiments with simulated images, with the results summarized in Table 3.5.

TABLE 3.4 (Real Scenes) Precision and Recall of Retrieving Relevant Literals for Constructing Answers to Questions With and Without Using the Learned Axioms for Reasoning. Using the Learned Axioms Significantly Improves the Ability to Provide Accurate Explanations in All but One Type of Query

Query Type	**Precision**		**Recall**	
	Without	**With**	**Without**	**With**
Plan description	78.5%	100%	67.5%	100%
Why X?	76.3%	95.3%	66.8%	95.3%
Why not X?	96.6%	96.6%	64%	100%
Why belief Y?	96.7%	99%	95.6%	99.2%

TABLE 3.5 (Simulated Scenes) Precision and Recall of Retrieving Relevant Literals for Constructing Answers to Questions With and Without Reasoning with Learned Axioms. Using the Learned Axioms Significantly Improves the Ability to Provide Accurate Explanations for All Four Types of Queries

Query Type	**Precision**		**Recall**	
	Without	**With**	**Without**	**With**
Plan description	70.8%	100%	58%	100%
Why X?	65.6%	93%	57%	93%
Why not X?	90.5%	96.4%	65.2%	100%
Why belief Y?	92.7%	98.4%	90.3%	99.2%

Tables 3.4 and 3.5 show that for all but one type of question (i.e., counterfactual) posed about real world scenes, the precision and recall of relevant literals (for constructing explanations) were higher when the learned axioms were used for reasoning compared with the baseline (which did not use these learned axioms). The improvement in performance was particularly pronounced when the robot had to answer certain types of questions about certain types of scenes (e.g., justification of action choices). For certain types of questions (e.g., about specific beliefs), the precision and recall rates were reasonable even when the learned axioms were not included. This is because not all the learned axioms were needed to answer each question. When the learned axioms were used for reasoning, errors were rare and corresponded to additional literals being included in the explanation (i.e., over-specified explanations). Enabling reasoning and learning to inform each other thus resulted in more accurate relational descriptions of decisions and beliefs in response to different types of questions. These results support **H2**.

CONCLUSIONS

The architecture described in this paper is a step towards greater transparency in reasoning and learning for integrated robot systems. The architecture encodes the principle of stepwise refinement to leverage the complementary strengths of non-monotonic logical reasoning with commonsense domain knowledge, data-driven learning from a limited set of examples, and the inductive learning of previously unknown axioms governing domain dynamics. After the designer provides the domain-specific information, then planning, diagnostics, and execution are automated. In addition, the interplay between representation, reasoning, and learning is used to embed the principles of explainable agency, enabling a robot to reliably and efficiently construct and provide on-demand relational descriptions of its decisions and beliefs in response to different types of questions. Experimental results described in this chapter, and those described in other related publications (Sridharan & Meadows 2019; Mota, Sridharan, & Leonardis 2021), demonstrate the smooth transfer of control and relevant knowledge between components of the architecture, confidence in the correctness of the robot's behavior, and the applicability of the underlying methodology to different domains.

Our architecture opens up multiple directions of future work. For example, we will further explore how the interplay between representation, reasoning, and learning can be leveraged to support explainable agency in one or more robots assisting humans in dynamic domains. In addition, we will conduct experimental studies with human participants evaluating the quality of our explanations, and use the feedback from these participants to make revisions of our architecture and algorithms. Furthermore, we will investigate whether our architecture can be extended to consider social norms while generating explanations of the decisions and beliefs of a robot assisting humans in complex domains.

ACKNOWLEDGMENTS

This work is the result of research threads pursued in collaboration with Tiago Mota, Heather Riley, Ben Meadows, Rocio Gomez, Michael Gelfond, Jeremy Wyatt, and Shiqi Zhang. This work was supported in part by the U.S. Office of Naval Research Science of Autonomy Awards N00014-13-1-0766, N00014-17-1-2434 and N00014-20-1-2390, the Asian Office of Aerospace Research and Development award FA2386-16-1-4071, and the U.K. Engineering and Physical Sciences Research Council award EP/S032487/1. All conclusions are those of the author.

REFERENCES

Anjomshoae, S., Najjar, A., Calvaresi, D., & Framling, K. (2019). Explainable agents and robots: Results from a systematic literature review. In *Proceedings of the Eighteenth International Conference on Autonomous Agents and Multiagent Systems* (pp. 1078–1088). Montreal, Canada: International Foundation for Autonomous Agents and Multiagent Systems.

Assaf, R., & Schumann, A. (2019). Explainable deep neural networks for multivariate time series predictions. In *Proceedings of the Twenty-Eighth International Joint Conference on Artificial Intelligence* (pp. 6488–6490). Macao, China: ijcai.og.

Balai, E., Gelfond, M., & Zhang, Y. (2013). Towards answer set programming with sorts. *Proceedings of the Twelfth International Conference on Logic Programming and Nonmonotonic Reasoning* (pp. 135–147). Corunna, Spain: Springer.

Borgo, R., Cashmore, M., & Magazzeni, D. (2018). Towards providing explanations for ai planner decisions. In D.W. Aha, T. Darrell, P. Doherty, & D. Magazzeni (Eds.) *Explainable Artificial Intelligence: Papers from the IJCAI Workshop.*

Chakraborti, T., Sreedharan, S., & Kambhampati, S. (2018). Explicability versus explanations in human-aware planning. In *Proceedings of the Seventeenth International Conference on Autonomous Agents and Multiagent Systems* (pp. 2180–2182). Stockholm, Sweden: International Foundation for Autonomous Agents and Multiagent Systems.

de Kleer, J., & Williams, B. C. (1987). Diagnosing multiple faults. *Artificial Intelligence, 32*, 97–130.

Ferrand, G., Lessaint, W., & Tessier, A. (2006). Explanations and proof trees. *Computing and Informatics, 25*, 1001–1021.

Fox, M., Long, D., & Magazzeni, D. (2017). Explainable planning. In D.W. Aha, T. Darrell, M. Pazzani, D. Reid, C. Sammut, & P. Stone (Eds.) *Explainable Artificial Intelligence: Papers from the IJCAI Workshop.*

Friedman, M. (1974). Explanation and scientific understanding. *Philosophy, 71*(1), 5–19.

Gebser, M., Kaminski, R., Kaufmann, B., & Schaub, T. (2012). Answer set solving in practice. *Synthesis Lectures on Artificial Intelligence and Machine Learning, 6*(3), 1–238.

Gelfond, M., & Inclezan, D. (2013). Some properties of system descriptions of. *Journal of Applied Non-Classical Logics, 23*(1–2), 105–120.

Gomez, R., Sridharan, M., & Riley, H. (2021). What do you really want to do? Towards a theory of intentions for human-robot collaboration. *Annals of Mathematics and Artificial Intelligence, 89*, 179–208.

Koh, P. W., & Liang, P. (2017). Understanding black-box predictions via influence functions. In *Proceedings of the Thirty-Fourth International Conference on Machine Learning* (pp. 1885–1894). Sydney, Australia: PMLR 70.

Krizhevsky, A., Sutskever, I., & Hinton, G. E. (2012). ImageNet classification with deep convolutional neural networks. In *Proceedings of the Twenty-Sixth Annual Conference on Neural Information Processing Systems* (pp. 1106–1114). Lake Tahoe, NV.

Laird, J. E. (2012). *The Soar cognitive architecture.* MIT Press.

Langley, P., Meadows, B., Sridharan, M., & Choi, D. (2017). Explainable agency for intelligent autonomous systems. In *Proceedings of the Thirty-First AAAI Conference on Artificial Intelligence* (pp. 4762–4763). San Francisco, CA: AAAI Press.

LeCun, Y., Bottou, L., Bengio, Y., & Haffner, P. (1998). Gradient based learning applied to document recognition. *Proceedings of the IEEE, 86*, 2278–2324.

Miller, G. A. (1995). WordNet: A lexical database for English. *Communications of the ACM, 38*(11), 39–41.

Miller, T. (2019). Explanations in artificial intelligence: Insights from the social sciences. *Artificial Intelligence, 267*, 1–38.

Mota, T., & Sridharan, M. (2018). Incrementally grounding expressions for spatial relations between objects. In *Proceedings of the Twenty-Seventh International Joint Conference on Artificial Intelligence* (pp. 1928–1934). Stockholm, Sweden: ijcai.org.

Mota, T., & Sridharan, M. (2021). Answer me this: Constructing disambiguation queries for explanation generation in robotics. In *Proceedings of the IEEE International Conference on Development and Learning* (pp. 1–8). Beijing, China: IEEE Press.

Mota, T., Sridharan, M., & Leonardis, A. (2021). Integrated commonsense reasoning and deep learning for transparent decision making in robotics. *Springer Nature CS, 2*(242), 1–18.

Norcliffe-Brown, W., Vafeais, E., & Parisot, S. (2018). Learning conditioned graph structures for interpretable visual question answering. In *Proceedings of the Thirty-First Annual Conference on Neural Information Processing Systems* (pp. 8344–8353). Montreal, Canada.

Read, S. J., & Marcus-Newhall, A. (1993). Explanatory coherence in social explanations: A parallel distributed processing account. *Personality and Social Psychology, 65*(3), 429.

Ribeiro, M., Singh, S., & Guestrin, C. (2016). Why should I trust you? Explaining the predictions of any classifier. In *Proceedings of the Twenty-Second ACM SIGKDD International Conference on Knowledge Discovery and Data Mining* (pp. 1135–1144). San Francisco, CA: ACM Press.

Seegebarth, B., Müller, F., Schattenberg, B., & Biundo, S. (2012). Making hybrid plans more clear to human users: A formal approach for generating sound explanations. In *Proceedings of the Twenty-Second International Conference on Automated Planning and Scheduling* (pp. 225–233). São Paulo, Brazil: AAAI Press.

Someya, Y. (1998). Lemma list for English language.

Sreedharan, S., Kulkarni, A., & Kambhampati, S. (2022a). *Explainable human-AI interaction: A planning perspective.* Springer.

Sreedharan, S., Kulkarni, A., & Kambhampati, S. (2022b). Explanation as model reconciliation. In *Explainable Human-AI Interaction: A Planning Perspective* (pp. 59–80). Springer.

Sridharan, M., & Meadows, B. (2018). Knowledge representation and interactive learning of domain knowledge for human-robot collaboration. *Advances in Cognitive Systems, 7*, 77–96.

Sridharan, M., & Meadows, B. (2019). Towards a theory of explanations for human-robot collaboration. *Kunstliche Intelligenz, 33*(4), 331–342.

Sridharan, M., & Mota, T. (2023). Towards combining commonsense reasoning and knowledge acquisition to guide deep learning. *Autonomous Agents and Multi-Agent Systems, 37*(1), 4.

Sridharan, M., Gelfond, M., Zhang, S., & Wyatt, J. (2019). REBA: A refinement-based architecture for knowledge representation and reasoning in robotics. *Journal of Artificial Intelligence Research, 65*, 87–180.

Winston, P. H., & Holmes, D. (2018). *The Genesis Enterprise: Taking artificial intelligence to another level via a computational account of human story understanding* (Computational Models of Human Intelligence Report 1). Computer Science and Artificial Intelligence Laboratory, Center for Brains, Minds, and Machines, Massachusetts Institute of Technology.

Yi, K., Wu, J., Gan, C., Torralba, A., Kohli, P., & Tenenbaum, J. B. (2018). Neural-symbolic VQA: Disentangling reasoning from vision and language understanding. In *Proceedings of the Thirty-First Annual Conference on Neural Information Processing Systems* (pp.1039–1050). Montreal, Canada.

CHAPTER 4

Explanation as Question Answering Based on User Guides

Ashok Goel, Vrinda Nandan, Eric Gregori, Sungeun An, and Spencer Rugaber

Design Intelligence Laboratory, School of Interactive Computing, Georgia Institute of Technology, Atlanta, GA, USA

INTRODUCTION, BACKGROUND, AND GOALS

AI research on explanation has a long history that dates at least as far back as the rise of expert systems in the 1960s, e.g., DENDRAL (Lindsay et al. 1993). Mueller et al. (2019) provide a recent and comprehensive review of this research. One of the key ideas to emerge out of this early research was the importance of the explicit representation of knowledge of the design of an AI system (Chandrasekaran & Swartout 1991; Chandrasekaran & Tanner 1989): An explicit representation of the design knowledge of an AI system enables the generation of explanations of the tasks it accomplishes, the domain knowledge it uses, as well as the methods that use the knowledge to achieve the tasks. This raised the question of how this design knowledge can be identified, acquired, represented, stored, accessed, and used for generating explanations. One possible answer was to endow the AI agent with meta-knowledge of its own design (e.g., Goel et al. 1996) and enable the agent to generate explanations through introspection of its meta-knowledge. However, much of AI research on expert systems collapsed by the mid-1990s.

DOI: 10.1201/9781003355281-4

Starting in the 1970s, AI research on explanation also encompassed intelligent tutoring systems (Buchanan 2006). Indeed, in the 1990s, given the collapse of AI research on expert systems, the focus of AI research on explanation shifted to intelligent tutoring systems. Unlike the design stance towards explanations adopted by the research on expert systems, research on tutoring systems took a strongly human-centered perspective. This view emphasized the users and the uses of explanations (e.g., Woolf 2007). For example, Graesser, Baggett, and Williams (1996) describe question-answering as a basic mechanism for generating explanations in intelligent tutoring systems, where the answers to the questions meet the requirements and expectations of the human users, and Aleven and Koedinger (2002) present explanations of reasoning as a source of new knowledge and learning for the users. However, much of this work perhaps lay a little outside mainstream AI research.

Over the last several years, explanation has again entered mainstream AI research (e.g., Gunning & Aha 2019). This is in part because of advances in machine learning, such as deep learning, that have refocused attention on the need for interpretability and explainability of internal representations and processing in AI agents in general (Gilpin et al. 2018; Rudin 2019). However, explanation of knowledge-based AI systems is also important for reasons of fairness, transparency, accountability, trustworthiness, and human understanding and learning.

In this chapter, we take the two ideas from explanations in expert systems and tutoring systems mentioned above as our starting points for generating explanations in knowledge systems: (1) use of the knowledge of the design of an AI agent as the basis for generating explanations, and (2) human-centered question-answering as the basic mechanism for generation of explanations. They add a third idea to this mix: Given that most practical AI agents, for example almost all intelligent tutoring systems, come with a User Guide that contains knowledge about the domain, design and operation of the agent (Ko et al. 2011), might the User Guide act as a basis for generating explanations? Note that almost by definition, the User Guide contains information about many types of explanations that users want. For example, a User Guide for an AI agent typically contains information about the domain of the agent, the vocabulary for representing the domain knowledge, the tasks and subtasks the agent accomplishes (what it does), the knowledge and the data the agent uses (its basic components), the methods in the agent that use the knowledge to accomplish its tasks (how the agent accomplishes its tasks), as well as the operation of the agent (how to use the agent). However, few humans actually read the User Guide in any detail (Mehlenbacher et al. 2002; Novick & Ward 2006; Rettig 1991). Instead, most users want answers to their questions on demand, as and when needed. Thus, (3) we propose to use the User Guide to generate answers to users' questions.

In this chapter, we describe the use of a question-answering agent (called AskJill) for generating explanations about an interactive learning environment (named VERA) based on the latter's Users Guide. AskJill is intended to automatically answer users' questions and thereby explain VERA's domain, functioning, and operation. We also present a preliminary formative assessment of AskJill in VERA.

VERA, AN INTERACTIVE LEARNING ENVIRONMENT

The VERA project addresses the issues of availability, achievability, and quality of online education. Residential students in higher education have access to physical laboratories, where they conduct experiments and participate in research, thus discovering new knowledge grounded in empirical evidence and connecting it with their prior knowledge. Online learners do not have access to physical laboratories, which impairs the quality of their learning. Thus, we developed a Virtual Experimentation Research Assistant (VERA for short) for inquiry-based learning of scientific knowledge (An et al. 2020; 2021): VERA helps learners build conceptual models of complex phenomena, evaluate them through simulation, and revise the models as needed. VERA's capability of evaluating a model by simulation provides formative assessment on the model; its support for the whole cycle of model construction, evaluation, and revision fosters self-regulated learning. Given that residential students have only limited access to physical laboratories, VERA is also useful for blended learning. VERA is available online (https://vera.cc.gatech.edu) for free and public use.

For the domain of ecology, we have integrated VERA with the Smithsonian Institution's Encyclopedia of Life that is available as an open-source library and software (EOL; Parr et al. 2016). EOL's TraitBank supports ecological modeling in VERA in several ways: it provides (i) the ontology of conceptual relations for conceptual modeling, (ii) knowledge of specific relations among biological species in a given ecological system, and (iii) the parameters for setting up the simulations. Thus, in VERA, biological species are modeled using data directly retrieved from EOL such as lifespan, body mass, offspring count, reproductive maturity, etc. Given that the space of simulation parameters can be very large, and a learner may not know the "right" values for the parameters, once the learner sets up the conceptual model using the EOL digital library, VERA further uses EOL's knowledge of biological species to directly set initial values of the simulation parameters. The learner may then tweak the parameter values and experiment with them. Figure 4.1 illustrates the use of VERA to model the impact of a kudzu "bug" to moderate the impact of kudzu, an Asian invasive species, on the American hornbeam, a kind of tree common in the eastern half of the United States. In Figure 4.1(a), the learner interactively builds a conceptual model, and in Figure 4.1(b) VERA illustrates the results of an agent-based simulation of the model. In this case, the simulation results show that because of the introduction of the kudzu bug, the population of kudzu will decline over time and the American hornbeam will survive.

VERA uses agent-based simulations to provide formative assessment on the conceptual models. An AI compiler inside VERA understands enough of the syntax and semantics of both the conceptual models and agent-based simulations that it can automatically spawn the latter from the former. This is another example of learning assistance in VERA. This learning assistance enables both student scientists and citizen scientists to model complex phenomena without requiring expertise in the mathematics or mechanics of agent-based simulations. Further, VERA's support for the whole cycle of model construction, evaluation, and revision fosters self-regulated learning.

In 2019, the Smithsonian Institution started providing access to VERA directly through the main page on its EOL website (www.eol.org). This means that the hundreds of thousands of EOL users across the world each year, including learners and teachers as well as citizen and professional scientists, now have direct access to VERA. This also makes explanations of VERA's domain, functioning, and operation critically important.

USER GUIDE IN VERA

VERA's User Guide and table of contents are available on its website under the Help section. It includes a written guide describing how users can build and simulate ecological experiments on VERA, the tool's expected behavior, explanations for the vocabulary terms and parameters users can manipulate, and screenshots showing the tool's structure

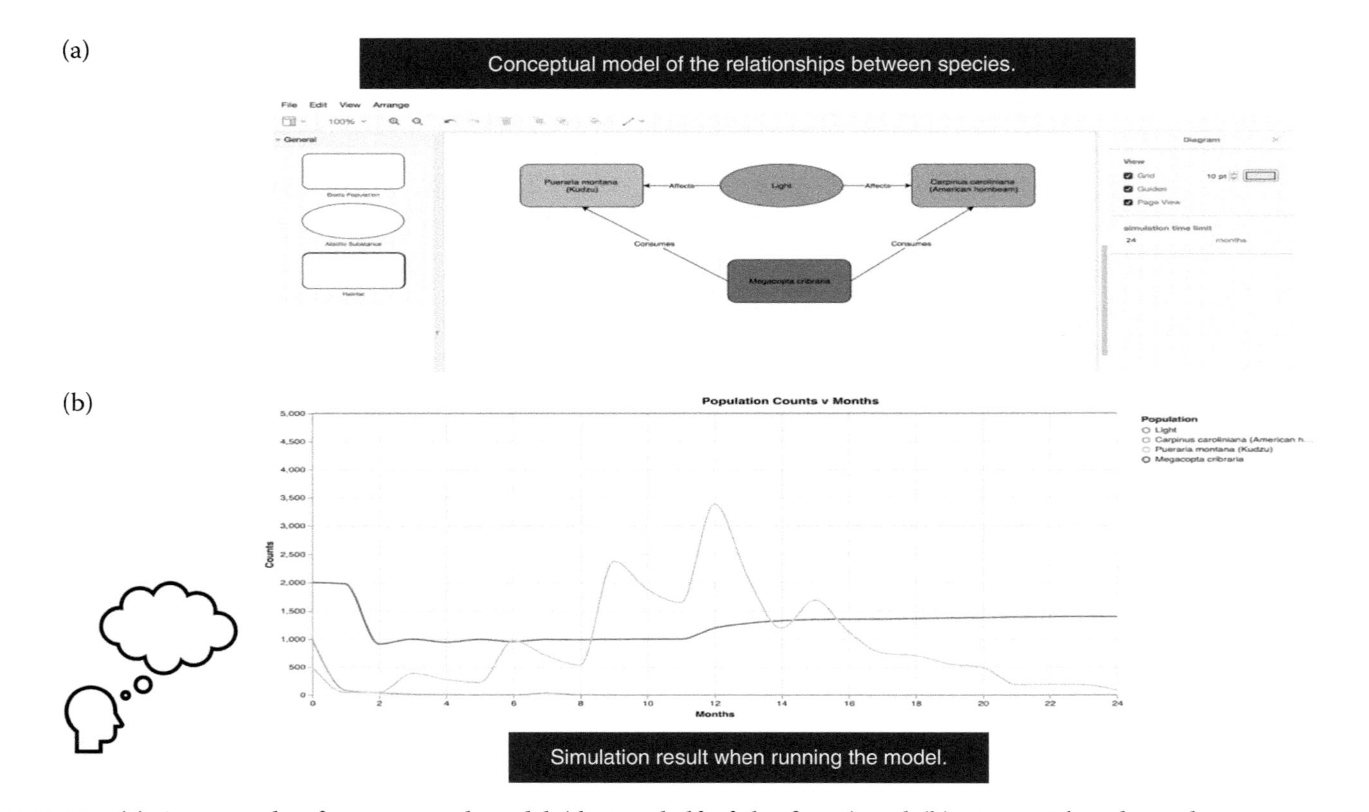

FIGURE 4.1 (a) An example of a conceptual model (the top half of the figure) and (b) its agent-based simulation automatically generated by VERA (the bottom half).

(screens and buttons). Specifically, the 27-page User Guide covers an introduction to VERA, system requirements, steps to access the tool, general approach to build and evaluate a conceptual model of an ecological system, how to use the VERA tool for modeling and simulation (including steps to create a project describing a phenomena and associated models to test various hypotheses), how to use the model editor to manage constituent components and their relationships, how to simulate a model, how to edit model parameters to manipulate results, and ways to get help on the tool.

The User Guide provides illustrative descriptions of the user's workflow on VERA. For example, in its "Getting to know the model editor" section, the User Guide provides an example of a "starter" conceptual model of a simple ecosystem composed of wolves, sheep, and grass, to walk the user through the steps needed to create a the "biotic population" components for each of the three populations. It also shows the user how to define the ecological relationships (destroys, produces, consumes, becomes, affects, can migrate to) between each set of components (e.g., wolves "consume" sheep, sheep "consume" grass), and simulate the model. The User Guide describes how users can set up, start, stop, reset the simulation and export resulting graphs. The User Guide also provides example parameter values showing how parameters can be initialized (Smithsonian's EOL supplies default values) and tuned (provides tuning values) to get the desired population behavior (shows resulting graphs for reference) in the simulation. Last but not the least, the User Guide provides definitions and explanations for commonly used model components (e.g., biotic substance, abiotic substance, and habitat) and their associated simulation parameters (e.g., some parameters for a biotic substance are lifespan, carbon biomass, minimum population, etc.).

ASKJILL, A QUESTION-ANSWERING AGENT

AskJill is a question-answering agent embedded in the VERA interactive learning environment that automatically answers users' questions and thereby explains VERA's domain, functioning, and operation. When a user first logs in on the VERA website, AskJill welcomes them and prompts them to ask their questions about VERA. The user can type their questions into the AskJill question-answering interface (integrated into the VERA website). AskJill provides accurate answers to the questions within the scope of the User Guide within a few seconds. Figure 4.2 shows examples of question-answering in AskJill.

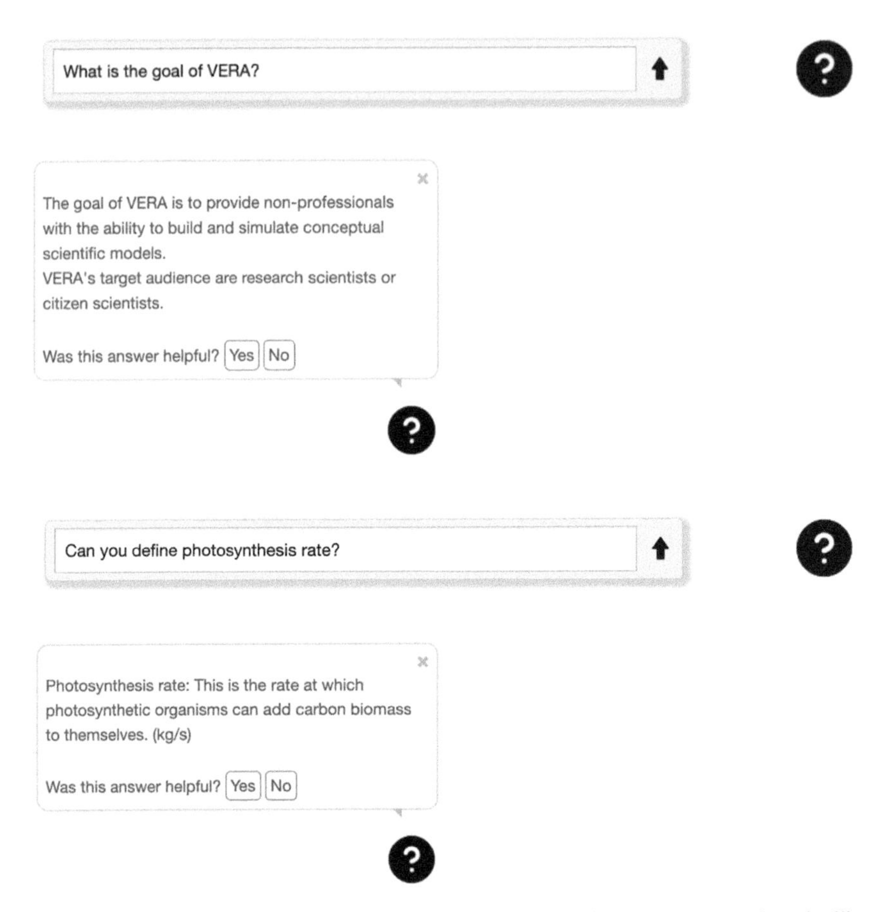

FIGURE 4.2 A couple of user questions to AskJill about VERA and AskJill's answers to the questions.

ASKJILL'S GENERATION OF AN ANSWER TO A QUESTION

Figure 4.3 shows AskJill's question-answering data flow diagram. After a user asks a question in VERA's AskJill interface, it is sent to the AskJill system via a REST API. Inside AskJill, the question is parsed, and then sent to a 2D hybrid classification system. The system contains a two-stage classification process (Goel 2020). The first is a pre-trained NLP-based intent classification layer that classifies each new question into one of the existing question categories based on user intents. The second is a semantic processing stage that uses the intent to select a rule-based query template. From the 2D hybrid classification system, a query is sent to the VERA's design knowledge database and a response is generated. The response generation system retrieves the associated query response and

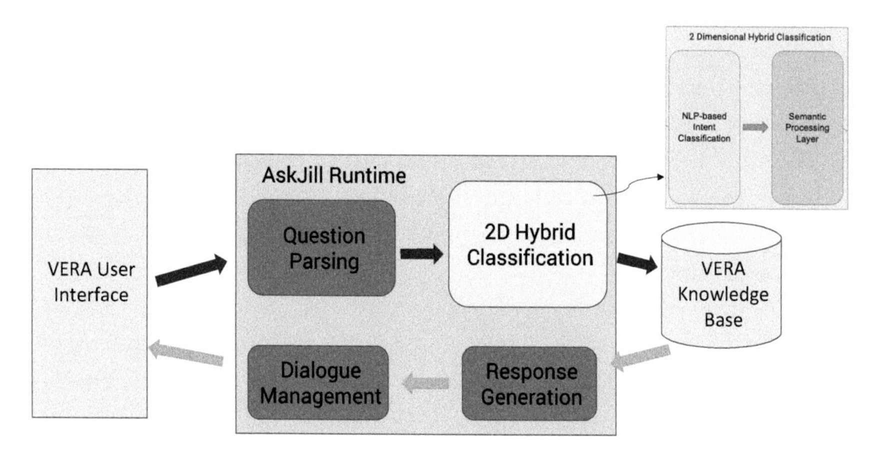

FIGURE 4.3 AskJill question-answering data flow diagram.

returns an answer if its confidence value exceeds the minimum threshold (97%). Finally, the dialogue management system post-processes the resulting response, converts it into a "human-like" natural language answer, and sends it back to AskJill in the VERA user interface. After answering, AskJill prompts the user to provide feedback, asking "Was this answer helpful," and stores the user feedback in her database. That feedback is subsequently used for retraining the agent. If AskJill is unable to answer a question, it can (a) gently redirect the conversation into its domain of competence by suggesting alternate topics associated with the questions it is trained on and/or (b) share relevant links to the User Guide.

AGENT SMITH: BUILDING ASKJILL FOR VERA'S USER GUIDE

AskJill evolved from our earlier work on the Jill Watson project (Goel & Polepeddi 2018) that automatically answered students' questions on discussion forums of online and hybrid classes. Agent Smith is an interactive generator for generating Jill Watson teaching assistants for different classes (Goel 2020; Goel, Sikka, & Gregori 2021): it combines knowledge-based AI, supervised machine learning, and human-in-the-loop machine teaching for training a Jill Watson assistant for a new class. Since AskJill for VERA's User Guide has the same architecture and algorithms as the original Jill Watson for class syllabi, we were able to reuse the Agent Smith generator to build the AskJill for VERA. Similar to previous Jill Watson applications, Smith builds a semantic memory for VERA's vocabulary, system requirements, structure, and tool behavior. It also generates a knowledge base consisting of user intents, keywords, and associated answers. Agent Smith then uses supervised learning to train a classifier to generate an AskJill for VERA. Reusing the Agent Smith technology allows us to train, retrain, and generate AskJill agents based on VERA's User Guide efficiently and easily. AskJill for VERA is encoded in the form of unique question templates related to goals, getting started, definitions, and how-to pointers, simulation parameter default values, and units.

While the rest of the technology from Jill Watson TA (teaching assistant) is reused, Agent Smith utilizes a brand-new set of template questions as well as VERA design knowledge base. A new set of template questions is needed because users pose different related questions (and underlying intents) to AskJill in VERA as compared to course related questions in Jill Watson TA. Similarly, a new knowledge base is needed because the AskJill agent for VERA is based on the User Guide, while the Jill Watson agent is based on course syllabus and schedule. Figure 4.4

what is the goal of {user}	goal
what is the purpose of {user}	goal
what is the objective of {user}	goal
what is the target audience for {user}	goal
who is {user} designed for	goal
who is {user} aimed for	goal
who is {user} targeted for	goal
who is {user} meant for	goal
who can use {user}	goal
who was {user} designed for	goal
what is {user} used for	goal
with what intention was {user} developed?	goal
what exactly is this {user}	goal

What is {object}	definition
Can you describe {object}	definition
Can you explain {object}	definition
What does {object} mean	definition
Can you define {object}	definition
What does {object} do	definition
Can you give an explanation for {object}	definition
What is {object} definition	definition
What is the definition of {object}	definition
How does {object} work	definition
What is {object} made up of	definition
what is the impact of {object}	definition
what does changing {object} do	definition
what happens if I change {object}	definition

How do I {object}	howdoi
Where do I find the {object}	howdoi
How can a model be {oject}	howdoi
How do I update {object}	howdoi
How can a model be {object}	howdoi
How do I change my {object}	howdoi
how do I use {object}	howdoi

where can I find {user}	gettingstarted
where are the {user}	gettingstarted
where do I start	gettingstarted
where do I begin	gettingstarted
how do I start	gettingstarted
how do I begin	gettingstarted
how do I get started	gettingstarted
what do I do first	gettingstarted
what do I do to begin	gettingstarted
what do I do to start	gettingstarted
what do I do to get started	gettingstarted
where can I find the getting started guide	gettingstarted
where is the getting started guide	gettingstarted
how do I access {user}	gettingstarted
how do I login to {user}	gettingstarted
where do I login to {user}	gettingstarted
how do I get started using {user}	gettingstarted
who all can use {user}	gettingstarted

FIGURE 4.4 Some examples of Agent Smith Question Templates for VERA Q&A AskJill Agent.

shows an example of the question templates used for training AskJill in VERA. Agent Smith projects the templates onto the VERA ontology and generates the training dataset. The AskJill agent uses the trained model for run-time question answering. Over time, as the authors collect user feedback and analyze missed questions, they can expand the training dataset and retrain AskJill enabling it to answer more and more questions. As a by-product of developing, testing, and training the AskJill Q&A agent, we identified definitions and parameters that were initially missing in the User Guide. We have since updated the User Guide to include those missed aspects.

EVALUATION OF ASKJILL IN VERA

We collected AskJill user data both during its use in an introduction to biology class at Georgia Tech, as well as from citizen scientists discovering VERA through Smithsonian's website or while browsing the Internet (An et al. 2020, 2021). Currently, AskJill can answer questions belonging to seven categories (intents) of questions, shown in Figure 4.5.

Figure 4.6 shows examples of a human-generated question from each question category above as well as AskJill's responses. The current training data set consists of 3,053 questions containing both the actual user questions and anticipated questions from the User Guide.

Given that Agent Smith automatically generated the training data set using a combination of template questions and relevant keywords, we also tested for the grammatical correctness of the generated training dataset. Out of 3,053 questions, 2,907 or 95.2% were accurate. The remaining 4.8% of questions were not grammatically correct but AskJill was still able to resolve the associated intents and answer them correctly. Figure 4.7 shows our validation results for the current training question set (3,053 questions): 100% of the agent-generated responses that are

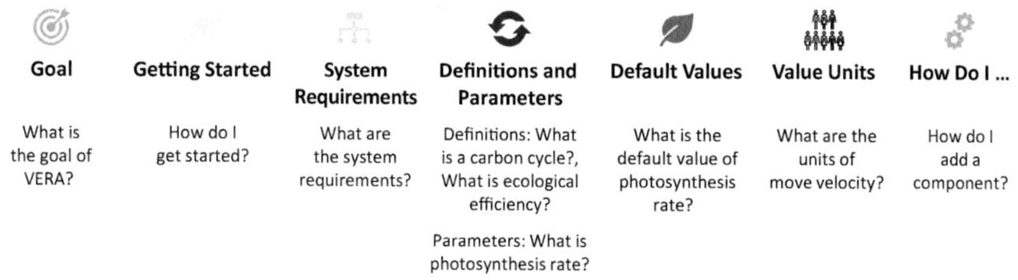

Goal	Getting Started	System Requirements	Definitions and Parameters	Default Values	Value Units	How Do I ...
What is the goal of VERA?	How do I get started?	What are the system requirements?	Definitions: What is a carbon cycle?, What is ecological efficiency? Parameters: What is photosynthesis rate?	What is the default value of photosynthesis rate?	What are the units of move velocity?	How do I add a component?

FIGURE 4.5 User Intent (question) categories on AskJill.

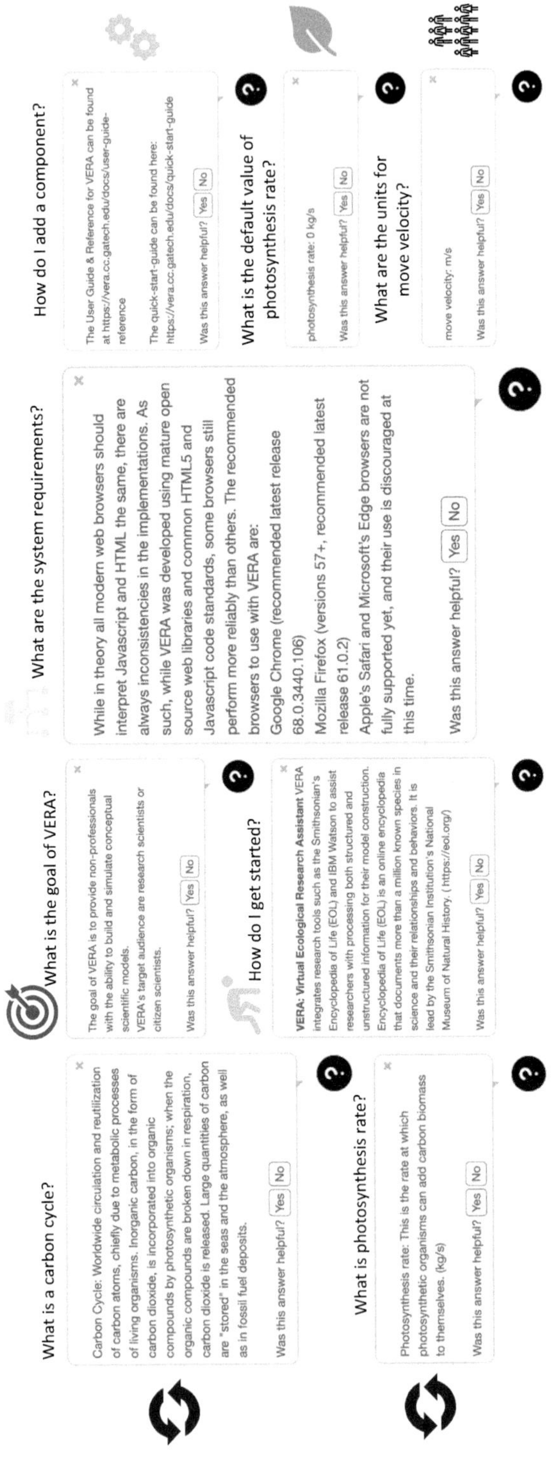

What is a carbon cycle?

Carbon Cycle: Worldwide circulation and reutilization of carbon atoms, chiefly due to metabolic processes of living organisms. Inorganic carbon, in the form of carbon dioxide, is incorporated into organic compounds by photosynthetic organisms; when the organic compounds are broken down in respiration, carbon dioxide is released. Large quantities of carbon are "stored" in the seas and the atmosphere, as well as in fossil fuel deposits.

Was this answer helpful? Yes No

What is photosynthesis rate?

Photosynthesis rate: This is the rate at which photosynthetic organisms can add carbon biomass to themselves. (kg/s)

Was this answer helpful? Yes No

What is the goal of VERA?

The goal of VERA is to provide non-professionals with the ability to build and simulate conceptual scientific models.
VERA's target audience are research scientists or citizen scientists.

Was this answer helpful? Yes No

How do I get started?

VERA: Virtual Ecological Research Assistant VERA integrates research tools such as the Smithsonian's Encyclopedia of Life (EOL) and IBM Watson to assist researchers with processing both structured and unstructured information for their model construction. Encyclopedia of Life (EOL) is an online encyclopedia that documents more than a million known species in science and their relationships and behaviors. It is lead by the Smithsonian Institution's National Museum of Natural History. (https://eol.org/)

Was this answer helpful? Yes No

What are the system requirements?

While in theory all modern web browsers should interpret Javascript and HTML the same, there are always inconsistencies in the implementations. As such, while VERA was developed using mature open source web libraries and common HTML5 and Javascript code standards, some browsers still perform more reliably than others. The recommended browsers to use with VERA are:
Google Chrome (recommended latest release 68.0.3440.106)
Mozilla Firefox (versions 57+, recommended latest release 61.0.2)
Apple's Safari and Microsoft's Edge browsers are not fully supported yet, and their use is discouraged at this time.

Was this answer helpful? Yes No

How do I add a component?

The User Guide & Reference for VERA can be found at https://vera.cc.gatech.edu/docs/user-guide-reference

The quick-start-guide can be found here: https://vera.cc.gatech.edu/docs/quick-start-guide

Was this answer helpful? Yes No

What is the default value of photosynthesis rate?

photosynthesis rate: 0 kg/s

Was this answer helpful? Yes No

What are the units for move velocity?

move velocity: m/s

Was this answer helpful? Yes No

FIGURE 4.6 Human-generated questions and AskJill's agent-generated answers.

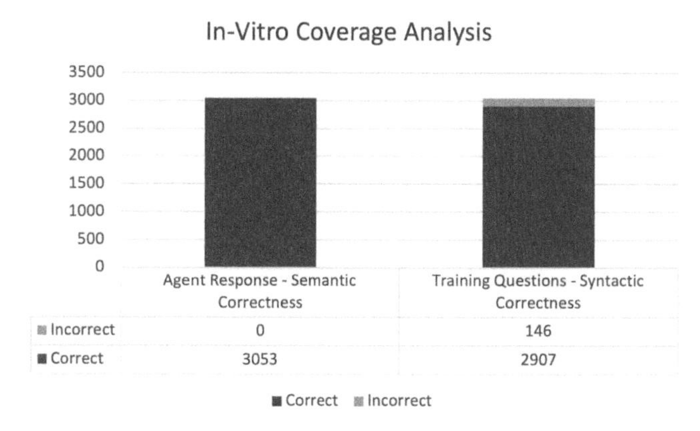

FIGURE 4.7 Agent response semantic correctness and training question syntactic correctness.

semantically correct. It also shows the split between syntactically correct and incorrect agent-generated questions.

We have also collected a small data set consisting of in-situ observations. Figure 4.8 shows a comparison of data collected from eight users, including external users as well as members of our research laboratory. AskJill correctly answered 19 out of 31 unique questions for all users. They measured user satisfaction using the integrated feedback prompt (Was this answer helpful?) built into the agent's interface and validated that the users confirmed (in some cases there was no feedback) that the correctly answered responses were indeed helpful to the user. Out of the 12 questions that were not answered correctly, a majority are related to simulation parameters, simulation properties, and how-to information specific to a given simulation and thus were outside the competence of AskJill (only 1 out of 12 questions is related to a missed definition). Taking the user feedback a step further, we also revised the

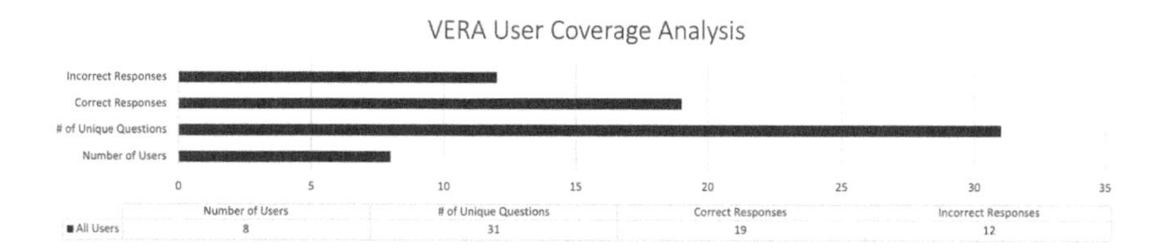

FIGURE 4.8 The bar plots show the correct vs incorrect responses (includes "I do not know"), the number of unique user questions, and the total number of users.

VERA User Guide to include answers to previously unanswered questions. The closed-loop process has resulted in significant improvements (i.e., adding information related to missed questions to the VERA knowledge domain, updating the User Guide, and retraining AskJill to expand its question-answering abilities) to the entire VERA and AskJill pipeline.

DISCUSSION

As Mueller et al. (2019) observe, explanations can be of multiple types. Tanner, Keuneke, and Chandrasekaran (1993) specifically distinguish between explanations of a phenomenon in the world and self-explanations about an agent's own design. The VERA interactive learning environment, for example, helps users generate explanations of ecological phenomena, such as the effect of the kudzu bug on the growth of kudzu in the southeast USA; in contrast, AskJill, the question-answering agent embedded in VERA, generates explanations about VERA's domain, design, and operation.

Generation of explanations of an AI agent typically requires specification and encoding of knowledge of the agent's design (Chandrasekaran & Swartout 1991; Chandrasekaran & Tanner 1989). In contrast, AskJill generates answers to a user's questions about an AI agent based on its User Guide, which, for fielded AI agents comes for "free." To put it another way, we recast explanation of practical AI agents as an interactive User Guide for answering users' questions. A corollary here is that we seek to identify the design knowledge a User Guide must contain to act as a basis for generating explanations.

While searching the User Guide for the specific information can be laborious and tedious, each information source has its own trade-offs. On one hand, the AskJill agent provides just-in-time, curated, and accurate answers to the user's questions. On the other, we expect the User Guide to offer its readers an opportunity to ponder and deepen their understanding as they search for some specific information and inadvertently discover new knowledge (including context and motivation) due to the inherent differences in the User Guide's structure and format (i.e., system diagrams, relationship tables, UI screenshots, related content, and references).

While our approach enables general-purpose explanations, it does not afford explanations of specific instances of reasoning and action by the AI agent. Thus, this approach likely has to be complemented with an episodic approach that relies on specific cases of decision making. Indeed, the case-based reasoning research community has developed several schemes for case-based explanation of decision making (Leake & McSherry 2005). In our work along these lines, we used meta-cases to capture derivational traces in an earlier interactive learning environment and used the meta-cases to explain the agent's decision making (Goel & Murdock 1996). A future version of AskJill may similarly keep a derivational trace of VERA's decision making and augment its explanatory capability based on a replay of the derivational trace.

Nevertheless, even in its current form, our approach provides insight into specific episodes of decision making both by explaining the vocabulary and the general mechanism of decision making. Consider again the explanation of decisions about the values of the simulation parameters in a specific episode of VERA's agent-based simulation. While AskJill cannot explain why the parameter values led to the specific simulation results in the given episode, it can and does explain each simulation parameter, the role it plays in the simulation, as well as the general mechanism of the agent-based simulation.

As mentioned earlier, AskJill builds on our earlier work on the Jill Watson project (Goel & Polepeddi 2018) that automatically answers students' questions on discussion forums of online and hybrid classes. One of the main reasons for the success of Jill Watson is that it took a very human-centric approach: it was trained to answer questions that students had actually asked in online discussion forums over a few years. However, Jill Watson answered questions based on course materials such as class syllabi and schedule. By answering questions based on VERA's Users Guide, AskJill generalizes the approach.

SUMMARY AND CONCLUSIONS

Explanation of an AI agent requires knowledge of its domain, design, and operation. Acquiring, representing, accessing, and using this design knowledge for generating explanations is challenging. However, almost all practical AI products and services come with a Users Guide that explains both how the product works and how to use the product. This is especially true for AI agents that actually get fielded in real settings and used by real users. Thus, we described the design of a question-answering agent (AskJill) that relies on the User Guide to an interactive learning environment (VERA) to explain its domain, functioning, and operation. This means that general explanations of the design of an AI agent now can be generated for "free," without requiring any special encoding of knowledge of the agent's design.

ACKNOWLEDGMENTS

Research on the VERA project is funded by an US NSF BigData Grant #1636848 and US NSF AI Institutes Grant #2112532. Both Jill Watson and AskJill use IBM's Watson platform for intent classification; the authors thank IBM for its support for our work. The authors also thank our collaborators on the VERA project, including Dr. Jennifer Hammock at Smithsonian Institution and Dr. Emily Weigel at Georgia Tech.

REFERENCES

Aleven, V., & Koedinger, K. (2002). An effective metacognitive strategy: Learning by doing and explaining with a computer-based cognitive tutor. *Cognitive Science, 26*(2), 147–179.

An, S., Bates, R., Hammock, J., Rugaber, S., Weigel, E. & Goel, A. (2020). Scientific modeling using large scale knowledge. In *Proceedings of the Twenty-First International Conference on AI in Education* (pp. 20–24). Ifrane, Morocco: Springer.

An, S., Broniec, W., Rugaber, S., Weigel, E., Hammock, J., & Goel, A. (2021). Recognizing novice learner's modeling behaviors. In *Proceedings of the Seventeenth International Conference on Intelligent Tutoring Systems* (pp. 189–200). Springer. https://www.wikidata.org/wiki/Q21820634

Buchanan, B. (2006). A (very) brief history of artificial intelligence. *AI Magazine, 26*(4), 53–60.

Chandrasekaran, B., & Swartout, W. (1991). Explanations in knowledge systems: The role of explicit representation of design knowledge. *IEEE Expert, 6*(3), 47–49.

Chandrasekaran, B., & Tanner, M. (1989). Explaining control strategies in problem solving. *IEEE Intelligent Systems, 4*, 9–15.

Gilpin, L, Bau, D., Yuan, B., Bajwa, A., Spector, M., & Kagai, L. (2018). Explaining explanations: An overview of interpretability of machine learning. In *Proceedings of the Fifth IEEE Conference on Data Science and Advanced Analytics* (pp. 80–89). Turin, Italy: IEEE Press.

Goel, A. (2020). AI-powered learning: Making Education accessible, affordable, and achievable. *arXiv preprint arXiv:2006.01908.*

Goel, A., & Murdock, W. (1996). Meta-cases: Explaining case-based reasoning. In *Proceedings of the Third European Workshop on Case-Based Reasoning* (pp. 150–163). Lausanne, Switzerland: Springer.

Goel, A., & Polepeddi, L. (2018). Jill Watson. In C. Dede, J. Richards, & B. Saxberg (Eds.) *Learning Engineering for Online Education: Theoretical Contexts and Design-Based Examples.* New York, NY: Routledge.

Goel, A., Gomes, A., Grue, N., Murdock, W., Recker, M., & Govindaraj, T. (1996). Explanatory interfaces in interactive design environments. In *Proceedings of the Fourth International Conference on AI in Design* (pp. 1–20). Stanford, CA: Kluwer.

Goel, A., Sikka, H., & Gregori, E. (2021). Agent Smith: Teaching question answering to Jill Watson. *arXiv preprint arXiv:2112.13677.*

Graesser, A., Baggett, W., & Williams, K. (1996). Question-driven explanatory reasoning. *Applied Cognitive Psychology, 10*(7), 17–31.

Gunning, D. & Aha, D., (2019). DARPA's Explainable Artificial Intelligence (XAI) Program. *AI Magazine, 40*(2), 44–58.

Ko, A.J., Abraham, R., Beckwith, L., Blackwell, A., Burnett, M., Erwig, M., Scaffidi, C., Lawrance, J., Lieberman, H., Myers, B. & Rosson, M.B. (2011). The state of the art in end-user software engineering. *ACM Computing Surveys, 43*(3), 1–44.

Leake, D. & McSherry, D. (2005). Introduction to the special issue on explanation in case-based reasoning. *Artificial Intelligence Review, 24*(2), 103–108.

Lindsay, R., Buchanan, B., Feigenbaum, E., & Lederberg, J. (1993). DENDRAL: A case study in the first expert system for scientific hypothesis formation. *Artificial Intelligence, 61*(2), 209–261.

Mehlenbacher, B., Wogalter, M., & Laughery, K. (2002). On the reading of product owner's manuals: Perceptions and product complexity. In *Proceedings of the Forty-Sixth Human Factors and Ergonomics Society Annual Meeting* (pp. 730–734). Los Angeles, CA: SAGE Publications.

Mueller, S. T., Hoffman, R. R., Clancey, W., Emrey, A., & Klein, G. (2019). Explanation in human-AI systems: A literature meta-review, synopsis of key ideas and publications, and bibliography for explainable AI. *arXiv preprint arXiv:1902.01876.*

Novick, D., & Ward, K. (2006). Why don't people read the manual? In *Proceedings of the Twenty-Fourth Annual ACM International Conference on Design of Communication* (pp. 11–18). Myrtle Beach, SC: ACM Press.

Parr C., Wilson, N., Schulz, K., Leary, P., Hammock, J., Rice, J, Corrigan Jr., R. (2016). TraitBank: Practical semantics for organism attribute data. *Semantic Web, 7*(6), 577–588.

Rettig, M. (1991). Nobody reads documentation. *Communications of the ACM, 34*(7), 19–24.

Rudin, C. (2019). Stop explaining black box machine learning models for high stakes decisions and use interpretable models instead. *Nature Machine Intelligence, 1*, 206–215.

Tanner M., Keuneke A., & Chandrasekaran B. (1993). Explanation using task structure and domain functional models. In J. David, J. Krivine, & R. Simmons (Eds.), *Second Generation Expert Systems*. Berlin: Springer Science & Business Media.

Woolf, B. (2007). *Building intelligent interactive tutors: Student-centered strategies for revolutionizing e-learning.* Morgan Kaufmann Publishers.

CHAPTER 5

Interpretable Multi-Agent Reinforcement Learning with Decision-Tree Policies*

Stephanie Milani[1], Zhicheng Zhang[1], Nicholay Topin[1], Zheyuan Ryan Shi[1], Charles Kamhoua[2], Evangelos E. Papalexakis[3], and Fei Fang[1]

[1]*Carnegie Mellon University, Pittsburgh, PA, USA*
[2]*Army Research Laboratory, Adelphi, MD, USA*
[3]*University of California, Riverside, CA, USA*

* This book chapter extends a full paper that appeared in the European Conference on Machine Learning and Principles and Practice of Knowledge Discovery in Databases 2022 (Milani & Zhang, et al., 2022) by Springer Nature with the following novel contributions. First, we have significantly rewritten the abstract, background, and related work, which makes it more accessible to a general audience. This chapter incorporates more high-level insights and explanations of key equations. Second, we provide a more detailed explanation of the IVIPER and MAVIPER algorithms, making them easier to understand. This chapter includes intuition about when the IVIPER algorithm is useful, a more extensive description of the MAVIPER motivation, important implementation details for MAVIPER, and more. Third, we have added additional statistical analyses to validate the significance of the empirical results, including the performance and robustness. These analyses resulted in the addition of the fourth contribution: a series of tables to showcase the findings (Tables 5.1–5.6). Furthermore, it strengthened the conclusions of the conference paper by demonstrating the superior or comparable performance of MAVIPER and/or IVIPER with the baselines. Given the time passage between the publication of the book chapter and the ECML publication, this chapter also features an updated related work section.

DOI: 10.1201/9781003355281-5

MARKOV GAMES AND MULTI-AGENT REINFORCEMENT LEARNING ALGORITHMS

In multi-agent reinforcement learning, a collection of N agents act in an environment defined by a Markov game (Shapley 1953; Littman 1994). A Markov game consists of a set of states S describing all possible configurations for all agents, the initial state distribution $\rho : S \rightarrow [0, 1]$, and the set of actions $A_1, \ldots, A_N$ and observations $O_1, \ldots, O_N$ for each agent $i \in N$. Each agent aims to maximize its own total discounted expected return $R_i = \sum_{t=0}^{\infty} \gamma^t r_i^t$. Here, γ is the discount factor that prioritizes the relative importance of future rewards and r_i^t is the reward achieved by agent i at timestep t. Toward this goal, each agent selects actions using a policy π_{θ_i}: $O_i \rightarrow A_i$, which is a mapping from an agent's private observation space to actions. The collection of policies for all agents is a policy profile $\pi = (\pi_1, \ldots, \pi_N)$; a policy profile excluding agent i is π_{-i}. After the agents execute their actions, the environment produces the next state and a reward vector. The next state is determined according to the state transition function P: $S \times A_1 \times \ldots \times A_N \rightarrow S$; the reward vector is produced according to each agent's reward function r_i: $S \times A_i \rightarrow R, \ \forall \ i \in N$. Each agent receives its own reward r_i and a private observation, consisting of a vector of *features*, correlated with the state $o_i : S \rightarrow O_i$.

Multi-agent reinforcement learning algorithms broadly fall under two categories: value-based (Sunehag et al. 2017; Rashid et al. 2018; Son et al. 2019) and policy gradient (most commonly, actor-critic) (Lowe et al. 2017; Foerster et al. 2018; Li et al. 2019; Yu et al. 2021). Value-based methods often model each agent's Q-function in the form of $Q_i^{\pi}(o_i, a_i)$ and derive the policy π_i by greedily choosing the action with the highest Q-value for that observation. Given a policy profile π, agent i's value function is defined as:

$$V_i^{\pi}(s) = r_i + \gamma \sum_{s' \in S} P(s, \ \pi_1(o_1), \ldots, \pi_N(o_N), \ s') \, V_i^{\pi}(s'),$$

which computes the agent-specific quality of a state. Its state-action value function is:

$$Q_i^{\pi}(s, \ a_1, \ \ldots, \ a_N) = r_i + \gamma \sum_{s' \in S} P(s, a_1, \ \ldots, a_N, \ s') \, V_i^{\pi}(s'),$$

which computes the quality of an action at a given state.

In contrast, actor-critic methods directly model the policy π_i, often with a neural network. These techniques typically follow the centralized training and decentralized execution paradigm (Oliehoek, Spaan, & Vlassis 2008). Each agent's policy must only take as input its private observation o_i to ensure decentralized execution. However, agents may leverage information beyond their private observation during training. Commonly, each agent i uses a centralized critic network Q_i^{π}, which takes as input some state information x (including the observations of all agents) and the actions of all agents. The use of this centralized critic addresses the stationarity issue in multi-agent reinforcement learning: without access to the actions of other agents, the environment seems non-stationary from the perspective of any one agent (Lowe et al. 2017).

Policies can also be modeled by decision trees (McCallum 1997). A decision tree induction algorithm is a non-parametric supervised learning algorithm that visualizes a decision-making process through a flowchart-like model (Quinlan 1986). It recursively partitions the input space along a specific feature using a cutoff value, called a split. The result of these splits are axis-parallel partitions. Internal nodes are the intermediate partitions, and leaf nodes are the final partitions. Figure 5.1 depicts an example decision tree policy for a single agent in the context of reinforcement learning. When used to model policies for reinforcement learning, the internal nodes represent the features and values of the input state used by the agent to choose its action, and the leaf nodes correspond to chosen actions given some input state. In multi-agent reinforcement learning, the most straightforward use of decision

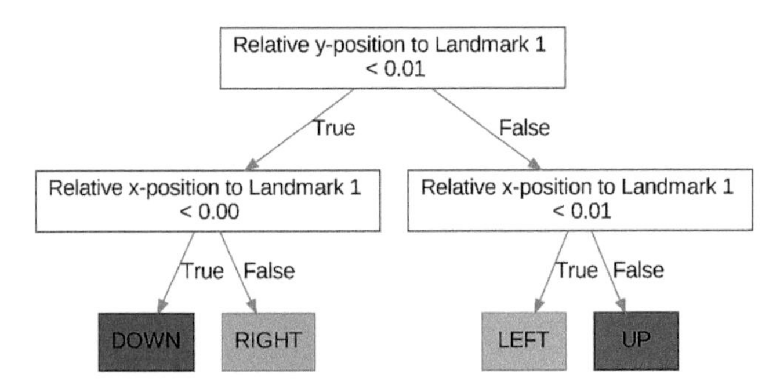

FIGURE 5.1 A decision tree of depth two learned by MAVIPER in a fully cooperative environment. The learned decision tree captures the expert's behavior of navigating to Landmark 1. First published in Milani et al. (2022) by Springer Nature. Reproduced with permission by Springer Nature.

tree policies applies one per agent, which means that the number of decision tree policies grows linearly with the number of agents.

Algorithm 1: Single-Agent VIPER

Input: (S, A, P, R), π^*, $Q^{\pi*}$, K, M

Output: A decision tree policy $\hat{\pi}$

1: Initialize dataset $D \leftarrow \emptyset$

2: Initialize policy $\hat{\pi}^0 \leftarrow \pi^*$

3: **for** iteration $m = 1$ to M **do**

4: Sample K trajectories according to: $D^m \leftarrow \{(s, \pi^*(s)) \sim d^{\hat{\pi}^{m-1}}\}$

5: Aggregate dataset $D \leftarrow D \cup D^m$

6: Resample dataset according to loss:
$$D' \leftarrow \{(s, a) \sim p((s, a)) \propto \tilde{l}(s)I[(s, a) \in D]\}$$

7: Train decision tree $\hat{\pi}^m \leftarrow TrainDecisionTree(D')$

8: **return** Best policy $\hat{\pi} \in \{\hat{\pi}^1, \cdots, \hat{\pi}^M\}$ on cross validation

---

EXTRACTING DECISION TREE POLICIES WITH SINGLE-AGENT VIPER

IVIPER and MAVIPER are based on single-agent VIPER (Bastani et al. 2018), which is a popular decision tree learning algorithm (Meng et al. 2020; Chen et al. 2021; Luss, Dhurandhar, & Liu 2022). Typically, researchers employ VIPER as a post-hoc explanation-generation method, in which the resulting decision tree only explains the guiding expert policy. Instead, this chapter uses the generated trees as the deployed policies. Crucially, VIPER extracts a decision tree given an *expert* policy trained using any single-agent reinforcement learning algorithm. It combines ideas from model compression (Buciluă, Caruana, & Niculescu-Mizil 2006; Hinton, Vinyals, & Dean 2015) and imitation learning (Abbeel & Ng 2004) – specifically, a variation of the classic DAGGER algorithm (Ross, Gordon, & Bagnell 2011). Different from DAGGER, VIPER uses the Q-function for the oracle and produces policies in the form of decision trees. This oracle guides the training of a decision tree policy. This section describes the VIPER algorithm.

As shown in Algorithm 1, VIPER trains a decision tree policy $\hat{\pi}^m$ in each iteration m; the final output is the best policy $\hat{\pi}_*$ among all iterations. In iteration m, it samples K trajectories: $\{(s, \hat{\pi}^{m-1}(s)) \sim d^{\hat{\pi}^{m-1}}\}$ following the decision tree policy trained at the previous iteration. Then, it uses the expert policy π_* to suggest actions for each visited state, leading to the data set $D^m = \{(s, \pi_*(s)) \sim d^{\hat{\pi}^{m-1}}\}$ (Algorithm 1, Line 4), where $d^{\hat{\pi}^{m-1}}$ is the distribution induced by the agent following its decision tree policy from the previous iteration. It therefore obtains expert-labeled data following the state visitation distribution induced by the decision tree policy. VIPER adds these relabeled experiences to a data set D consisting of experiences from previous iterations (Algorithm 1, Line 5). Let V^{π^*} and Q^{π^*} be the state value function and state-action value function given the expert policy π_*. Because the standard loss function for decision trees is not convex, VIPER does not optimize for it. Instead, VIPER resamples points $(s, a) \in D$ weighted according to:

$$\tilde{l}(s) = V^{\pi^*}(s) - \min_{a \in A} Q^{\pi^*}(s, a),$$

as in Line 6 in Algorithm 1. This resampling produces a new, weighted data set D’. Using CART (Breiman et al. 2017) to train a decision tree on D‘ is equivalent in expectation to training a decision tree with a potentially non-convex loss function. Single-agent VIPER forms the basis for the IVIPER and MAVIPER algorithms.

Algorithm 2: IVIPER for the Multi-Agent Setting

Input: (X, A, P, R), π^*, Q^*, K, M

Output: A decision tree policy profile $\hat{\pi} = (\hat{\pi}_1, \ldots, \hat{\pi}_N)$

1: **for** agent $i = 1$ to N **do**

2: Initialize data set $D_i \leftarrow \varnothing$ and policy $\hat{\pi}_i^0 \leftarrow \pi_i^*$

3: **for** iteration $m = 1$ to M **do**

4: Sample K trajectories according to: $D_i^m \leftarrow \{(x, \pi_1^*(o_1), \ldots \pi_N^*(o_N)) \sim d^{\hat{\pi}_i^{m-1}, \pi_{-i}^*}\}$

5: Aggregate dataset $D_i \leftarrow D_i \cup D_i^m$

6: Resample dataset according to loss:
$$D'_i \leftarrow \{(x, a) \sim p((x, a)) \propto \tilde{l}_i(x) I[(x, a) \in D_i]\}$$

7: Train decision tree $\hat{\pi}_i^m \leftarrow TrainDecisionTree(D'_i)$

8: Get best decision tree policy $\hat{\pi}_i^m \leftarrow BestPolicy(\hat{\pi}_i^1, \ldots, \hat{\pi}_i^M, \pi_{-i}^*)$

9: **return** Best policies for each agent $\hat{\pi} = (\hat{\pi}_1, \ldots, \hat{\pi}_N)$ on cross validation

IVIPER

Motivated by the success of single-agent reinforcement learning algorithms in the multi-agent reinforcement learning setting (Matignon, Laurent, & Le Fort-Piat 2012; Berner et al. 2019), IVIPER independently applies the single-agent VIPER algorithm to each agent, with a few critical changes. Algorithm 2 shows the full IVIPER pseudocode. At a high level, each agent independently trains a collection of decision tree policies, then selects the best policy from the collection. To account for the behavior of other agents, the expert policies of the other agents are used for environment rollouts.

The important changes for moving to the multi-agent setting are as follows. First, each agent i must have sufficient information for training its decision tree policy. As shown in Algorithm 2, Lines 2 and 4, each agent maintains its own data set of training tuples $D_i = \{x, a_1, \ldots, a\_N\}$. When using VIPER with multi-agent actor-critic methods that leverage a per-agent centralized critic network Q_i^{π}, we ensure that each agent's data set D_i contains, at a minimum, the observations and actions for all agents. The action for each other agent is provided by the expert policy corresponding to that agent $\pi_j^*(o_j)\ \forall\, j \neq i$. By giving each agent information about all other agents, IVIPER accounts for the influence of other agents on the environment. The use of a per-agent data set means that any data set-level operations are performed independently, on a per-agent basis.

Second, IVIPER accounts for important changes that emerge from moving from single-agent to multi-agent formalism. Specifically, when IVIPER samples and relabels trajectories for training each agent's decision-tree policy, it must sample from the distribution d induced by multiple agents acting in the environment. As a result, the distribution in Algorithm 2, Line 4, becomes $d^{\hat{\pi}_i^{m-1}, \pi_{-i}^*}$, which is induced by agent i's decision-tree policy at the previous iteration $\hat{\pi}_i^{m-1}$ and the expert policies of all other agents π_{-i}^*. Additionally, in Line 4, IVIPER relabels only the action for agent i because the other agents $-i$ choose their actions according to π_{-i}^*. This setup is equivalent to treating all other experts as part of the environment and using only a decision-tree policy for agent i.

Third, rather than considering only the actions of agent i, IVIPER incorporates the actions of all agents when resampling the data set (Algorithm 2, Line 6). If the multi-agent reinforcement learning algorithm uses a centralized critic $Q^{\pi}(s, a_1, \ldots, a_N)$, then it resamples points according to:

$$p((x, a_1, \ldots, a_N)) \propto \tilde{l}_i(x) I[(x, a_1, \ldots, a_N) \in D_i],$$

where

$$\tilde{l}_i(x) = V_i^{\pi^*}(x) - Q_i^{\pi^*}(x, a_i, a_{-i})|_{a_{-i}=\pi_j^*(o_j)\,\forall j \neq i}.$$

Note that IVIPER includes the actions of all other agents to select agent i's minimum Q-value from its centralized Q-function. In contrast, when applied to value-based methods, IVIPER more closely resembles single-agent VIPER. In Algorithm 2, Line 4, it is sufficient to store only o_i and a_i^*, where a_i^* is the action chosen by the expert using Q_i^*, in the data set D_i^m. Trajectories must still be sampled according to $\hat{\pi}_i^{m-1}$ and the Q-functions of the other agents Q_{-i}^*. To remove the reliance of the loss on the centralized critic, IVIPER uses the loss from single-agent VIPER in line 6:

$$\tilde{l}_i(s) = V_i^{\pi^*}(o_i) - \min_{a_i \in A_i} Q_i^{\pi^*}(o_i, a_i).$$

These algorithmic changes form the basis of the IVIPER algorithm. A helpful way to view this algorithm is as a transformation of the multi-agent learning problem into a single-agent one, in which other agents are folded into the environment. Since this algorithm is fully decentralized, agents may be trained in parallel. This approach is well suited for situations when only an interpretable policy for a single agent in a multi-agent setting is desired or agents do not need to *coordinate* with each other. As a motivating example of this algorithm's challenges with coordination, consider the case where two agents must split up to navigate to two different landmarks. These agents must coordinate to prevent the agents from navigating to the same landmark. With IVIPER, each agent is trained independently without consideration for what the other agent's resulting decision-tree policy will learn. As a result, the agents may learn to navigate to the same landmark. This problem of reliable coordination motivates the MAVIPER algorithm.

MAVIPER

MAVIPER is a novel algorithm for learning coordinated multi-agent decision tree policies in a centralized manner. For exposition, this section first describes MAVIPER in a fully cooperative setting, and then explains how to use MAVIPER for mixed competitive-cooperative settings. At a high level, MAVIPER jointly grows the trees – one for each agent – by predicting the behavior of the other agents in the environment using their anticipated trees. To train each decision tree policy, MAVIPER employs a novel resampling technique to find states that are critical for its interactions with other agents. Algorithm 3 depicts the full MAVIPER algorithm. Specifically, MAVIPER is built upon the following extensions to IVIPER that aim at addressing the issue of coordination.

Algorithm 3: MAVIPER (Joint Training)

Input: $(X, A, P, R), \pi^*, Q^*, K, M$
Output: A decision tree policy profile $\hat{\pi} = (\hat{\pi}_1, \ldots, \hat{\pi}_N)$

1: Initialize dataset $D \leftarrow \varnothing$ and policies $\hat{\pi}_i^0 \leftarrow \pi_i^*$ **for** agent $i = 1$ to N

2: **for** iteration $m = 1$ to M **do**

3: Sample K trajectories according to:
$$D^m \leftarrow \{(x, \pi_1^*(o_1), \ldots \pi_N^*(o_N)) \sim d^{\hat{\pi}_1^{m-1}, \ldots, \hat{\pi}_N^{m-1}}\}$$

4: Aggregate data set $D \leftarrow D \cup D^m$

5: **for** each agent i, resample D_i according to loss:
$$D'_i \leftarrow \{(x, a) \sim p((x, a)) \propto \tilde{l}_i(x) I[(x, a) \in D_i]\} \ \forall\, i \in N$$

6: Jointly train decision trees:
$$(\hat{\pi}_1^m, \ldots, \hat{\pi}_N^m) \leftarrow TrainJointTrees(D'_1, \ldots, D'_N)$$

7: **return** Best policies for each agent
$$\hat{\pi} = (\hat{\pi}_1, \ldots, \hat{\pi}_N) \in \{(\hat{\pi}_1^1, \ldots, \hat{\pi}_N^1), \ldots, (\hat{\pi}_1^M, \ldots, \hat{\pi}_N^M)\}$$

function TrainJointTrees

1: Initialize decision tree policies $\hat{\pi}_1^m, \ldots, \hat{\pi}_N^m$

2: **while** all trees are not at maximum depth

3: Grow one more level for agent i's tree $\hat{\pi}_i^m \leftarrow Build(\hat{\pi}_1^m, \ldots, \hat{\pi}_N^m, D_i)$

4: Move to the next agent $i \leftarrow (i + 1)\%N$

5: **return** decision trees $\hat{\pi}_1^m, \ldots, \hat{\pi}_N^m$

First, notice that the IVIPER loss treats the other agents as stationary experts. This assumption is problematic, as finding a decision tree policy that is consistent with the training set is NP-hard (Hancock et al. 1996): there is no guarantee that the learned decision tree policies will be optimal. As a result, the assumption that the decision tree policies of the other agents will align with the corresponding experts is unlikely to be true in practice. It is also worth mentioning that the training set may not fully represent the expert policies, making it even more challenging to align the decision tree policies with the experts' behavior.

To mitigate this issue, MAVIPER alters the resampling probability $p((x, a_1, \ldots, a_N))$ by focusing on the critical states where taking a joint action can make a difference. Using the insight that agents should care most about states in which there is a large gap between its worst-case performance and the expert performance, the loss function for each agent becomes:

$$\tilde{l}_i(x) = E_{a_{-i}}\left[Q_i^{\pi^*}(x, \pi_i^*(o_i), a_{-i}) - \min_{a_i \in A_i} Q_i^{\pi^*}(x, a_i, a_{-i})\right].$$

The first term in the loss measures the best-case performance of agent i, measured by the largest Q-value following the expert π_i^*. The second term measures the worst-case performance of agent i, measured by the smallest Q-value according to $Q_i^{\pi^*}$. The loss function then becomes the difference between the best-case and worst-case performance of agent i, rather than the difference between the average performance (calculated by $V_i^{\pi^*}(\cdot)$) and the worst-case performance. Furthermore, note that the expectation is taken over the actions of all other agents.

Second, rather than using the expert policies of all other agents to perform rollouts and collect new data, MAVIPER uses the decision tree policies $\hat{\pi} = (\hat{\pi}_1^{m-1}, ..., \hat{\pi}_N^{m-1})$ from the last iteration. Consequently, the distribution in Algorithm 3, Line 3, becomes $d^{\hat{\pi}_1^{m-1}, ..., \hat{\pi}_N^{m-1}}$. The goal of this change is to align more closely with the original DAGGER algorithm, where the idea is to aggregate a data set of inputs that the learned policy is likely to encounter during execution. Because there is typically some approximation error when constructing decision tree policies, the states encountered by following them will likely differ from those encountered by following the expert policies.

---

function Build $(\hat{\pi}_1^m, ..., \hat{\pi}_N^m, D_i)$

1: **for** each data point **do**

2: // will agent j's (projected) final decision tree policy predict its action correctly?

$$v_j \leftarrow I\,[Predict\,(\hat{\pi}_j^m, x) = a_j]\ \forall\, j \in N$$

3: // this data point is useful only if many agents' final decision-tree policies correctly predict their actions from it

if $\sum_{j=1}^{N} v_j < \tau$ **then** remove d from data set $D_i \leftarrow D_i \setminus \{(x, a)\}$

4: Calculate best next feature split for decision tree $\hat{\pi}_i^m$ using D_i

5: **return** decision tree $\hat{\pi}_i^m$

---

function Predict$(\hat{\pi}_j^m, x)$

1: Use x to traverse until leaf node $L(x)$

2: Train a projected final decision-tree policy

$\hat{\pi}_1^{‘} \leftarrow TrainDecisionTree\,(D’)$

3: **return** prediction: $\hat{\pi}_j^{‘}.\ predict\,(x)$

Third, MAVIPER adds a prediction module to increase the *joint* accuracy, which means that the predicted actions by most of the decision-tree policies align with the actions that the corresponding experts would take. This prediction module is utilized in the Build function, which is called when training the trees jointly, as detailed in the TrainJointTrees function. The goal of the prediction module is to incorporate predictions of the actions that the other decision trees might make at each split point during the tree-growing process. The Predict function shows this process.

The prediction module works as follows. MAVIPER evenly grows the trees using a breadth-first ordering to avoid biasing toward the result of any specific tree. Because the true decision tree policies are incomplete at the time of prediction, MAVIPER instead uses the output of another tree $\hat{\pi}'_J$ for the prediction. This decision tree is trained with the data set associated with the node for that prediction. Following the intuition that the correct prediction of one agent alone may not yield much benefit if the other agents are incorrect, the data set used for training the agent is filtered using the following rule. If the proportion of correct predictions for a data point is less than a predefined threshold τ, it is removed from the training data set for that node. The Build function shows this filtering process. MAVIPER then calculates the splitting criteria based on this modified data set and continues iteratively growing the tree. These changes comprise the MAVIPER algorithm for the fully cooperative setting.

This section now focuses on mixed competitive-cooperative settings, in which agents in a team share goals and require coordination with each other but encounter other agents or teams with potentially conflicting goals. In these settings, MAVIPER follows a similar procedure but applied on a per-team basis. More specifically, for a team Z, MAVIPER constrains the Build and Predict functions to make predictions for only the agents in the same team. Therefore, the loss in Algorithm 3, Line 5, takes the expectation over the joint actions for agents outside the team and becomes:

$$l_i(x) = E_{a_{-Z}}[Q_i^{\pi^*}(x, \ \pi_i^*(o_i), \ a_{-Z}) - Q_i^{\pi^*}(x, a_i, a_{-Z})].$$

This change is sufficient to move to the mixed competitive-cooperative setting.

There are a few additional implementation details worth mentioning. To optimize running speed, MAVIPER adopts a caching mechanism for the decision trees. This caching mechanism enables MAVIPER to avoid training a new decision tree for each data point being predicted in the Build function. To speed up the Predict function, MAVIPER initially gathers all the necessary predictions for a particular tree and then conducts a batched traversal to obtain the predictions. This optimization technique substantially reduces the need for multiple tree traversals, which leads to an improvement in efficiency.

These changes comprise the MAVIPER algorithm. Because MAVIPER explicitly accounts for the anticipated behavior of other agents in both the predictions and the sampling probability, it should better capture coordinated behavior.

EXPERIMENTS

This section investigates how well MAVIPER and IVIPER agents perform in a variety of environments. Because the goal is to learn high-performing yet interpretable policies, the quality of the trained policies is empirically evaluated in three multi-agent environments: two mixed competitive-cooperative environments and one fully cooperative environment. Agents are evaluated based on the performance of the decision tree policies because the goal is to deploy these policies in place of the expert ones. The hypotheses tested by the experiments are:

H1: MAVIPER and IVIPER learn decision-tree policies that achieve higher individual performance than the baselines.

H2: MAVIPER learns better coordinated decision-tree policies than IVIPER and the baselines.

H3: MAVIPER learns decision-tree policies that are more robust to different adversaries.

Since small decision trees are considered interpretable, the maximum depth is constrained to be at most 6. The expert policies used to guide the decision-tree training are generated by MADDPG (Lowe et al. 2017). The Pytorch (Paske et al. 2017) implementation is used for MADDPG: https://github.com/shariqiqbal2810/maddpg-pytorch. The experiments include comparisons to two baselines.

Fitted Q-Iteration

This baseline does not explicitly aim to imitate an expert; instead, it directly learns a Q-function and uses it to choose actions. Fitted Q-Iteration iteratively approximates the Q-function with a regression decision tree (Ernst, Geurts, & Wehenkel 2005). To account for continuous state values, the states are first heuristically discretized with 10 evenly spaced bins: $(-\infty, -1)$, $[-1, -.75)$, ..., $[.5, .75)$, $[.75, 1.)$, $(1, \infty)$. Each agent derives its policy by taking the action associated with the highest estimated Q-value for that input state.

Imitation DT

This baseline is a simple imitation learning algorithm. First, a data set is collected by running the expert policies for multiple episodes. Using this data set, each decision tree policy is trained independently. No resampling is performed. The observations for an agent are the features, and the actions for that agent are the labels.

The hyperparameters and the hyperparameter selection process can be found in Milani & Zhang et al. 2022. A high-performing MADDPG expert is trained for each environment, then each decision tree learning algorithm is run 10 times with different random seeds. All policies are evaluated after training by running 100 episodes. The algorithms are evaluated on three multi-agent particle world environments (Lowe et al. 2017), described below. Episodes terminate after $T = 25$ timesteps.

Physical Deception

In this mixed competitive-cooperative environment, a team of N defenders protect N targets from one adversary. One of the targets is the true target. This information is known to the defenders but not to the adversary. For these experiments, $N = 2$. During an episode, the defenders succeed if they split up to simultaneously cover all targets; the adversary succeeds if it reaches the true target during the episode. Covering and reaching targets is defined as being ε-close to a target for at least one timestep during the episode. The primary performance metric for this environment is the defenders' and adversary's success rate.

Cooperative Navigation

This fully cooperative environment consists of a team of N agents that must learn to cover all N targets while avoiding collisions with each other. For these experiments, $N = 3$. Agents succeed during an episode if they split up to simultaneously cover all targets without colliding. The primary performance metric is the summation of the distance of the closest agent to each target, for all targets. Low values of the metric indicate that the agents correctly learn to split up.

Predator–Prey

This environment variant involves a team of K slower, cooperating predators that chase M faster prey. There are $L = 2$ landmarks impeding the way. For these experiments, $K = M = 2$. Different from the original environment, the observation space of each agent is restricted to mostly consist of binarized relative positions and velocity (if applicable) of the landmarks and other agents in the environment. The primary performance metric is the number of collisions between predators and prey. For prey, lower is better as it means that the predators catch them less often; in contrast, for predators, higher is better.

INDIVIDUAL PERFORMANCE COMPARED TO EXPERTS

This section investigates whether a single agent can perform similarly when it adopts its decision-tree policy compared with its expert policy, in the setting where all other agents use expert policies. Given a decision tree policy profile $\hat{\pi}$ and the expert policy profile π^*, if agent i from team Z uses its decision tree policy, then the individual performance ratio is defined as:

$$\textit{Individual performance ratio} = E\left[U_i^{\pi_{-i}^*}\right] = \frac{U_Z(\hat{\pi}_i, \pi_{-i}^*)}{U_Z(\pi^*)},$$

where $U_Z(\cdot)$ is team Z's performance given the agents' policy profile (since the primary performance metric is at the team level). A performance ratio of 1 means that the decision-tree policies perform as well as the expert ones. A ratio of above 1 is possible because the comparison is between the performance, not the similarity, of the decision tree and expert policies. This set of experiments tests hypothesis **H1**. Figure 5.2 reports the mean individual performance ratio averaged over all trials and all agents in the team. MAVIPER and IVIPER defenders outperform the two baselines for all maximum depths in physical deception; however, MAVIPER and IVIPER adversaries appear indistinguishable from each other and from Imitation DT adversaries in physical deception. MAVIPER outperforms the other algorithms in cooperative navigation and predator–prey.

First looking at the adversaries, a one-way ANOVA was performed for each maximum depth to compare the effect of the four different decision tree training algorithms on the adversary's individual performance ratio

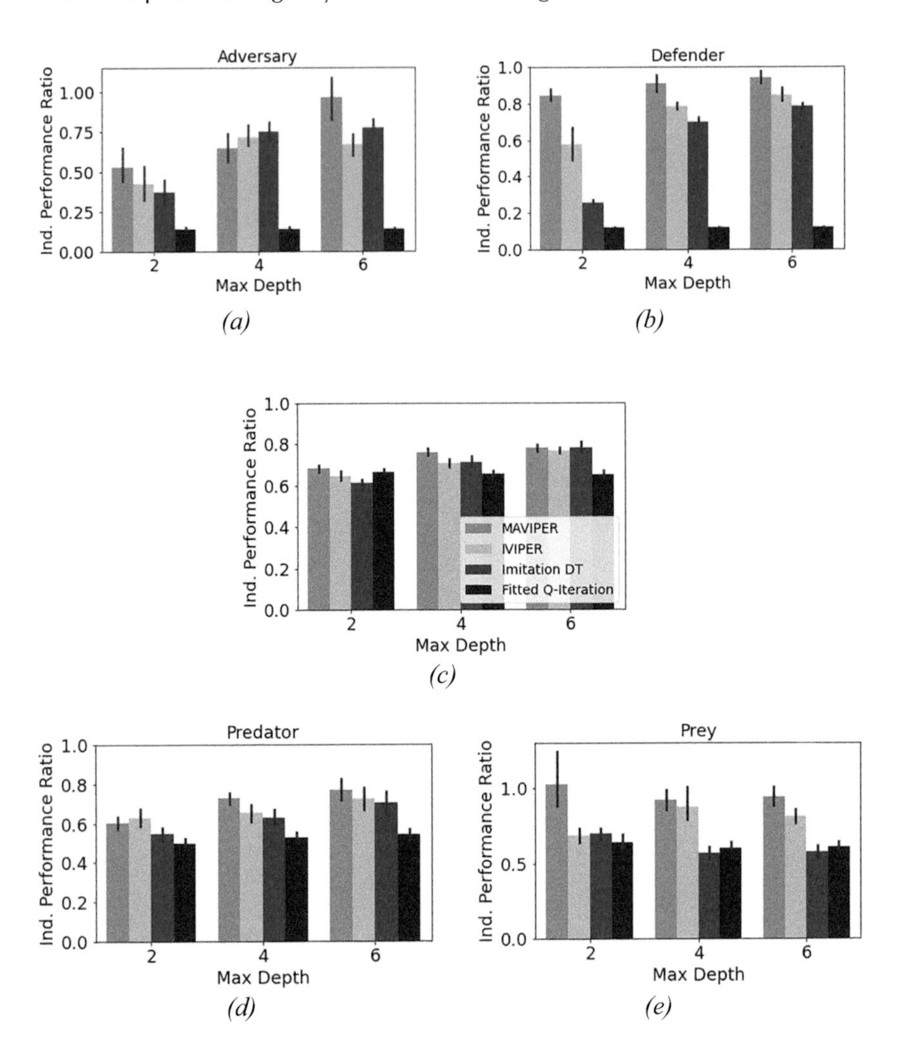

FIGURE 5.2 Individual performance ratio: relative performance when only one agent adopts a decision-tree policy. Higher is better. Error bars correspond to the 95% confidence interval. (First published in Milani et al. 2022 by Springer Nature. Reproduced with permission by Springer Nature.). *(a) Individual adversary performance, Physical Deception. (b) Individual defender performance, Physical Deception. (c) Individual agent performance, Cooperative Navigation. (d) Individual predator performance, Predator–Prey. (e) Individual prey performance, Predator–Prey.*

(Table 5.1, left side of the three rightmost columns). This test revealed a statistically significant difference in the individual performance ratio of the adversary between at least two groups for all maximum depths (maximum depth of 2: $F(3, 36) = 13.5623$, $p = 0.0000$; maximum

TABLE 5.1 Tukey's HSD Test Results Comparing the Average Individual Performance of the Adversary and Defender in the Physical Deception Environment. The Highest-Performing, Statistically Significant Results for Each Tree Depth (and the Corresponding p-Value) are in **Bold**. To Distinguish the Results, the Best-Performing Adversary is Denoted in **Underline**, and the Best-Performing Defender Is Denoted in **Italic** (If the Results Are Statistically Significant). Results Are Presented as: Predator, Prey. The α Level Is 0.05

Algorithm 1	Algorithm 2	Depth	Algorithm 1 Mean Adversary, Defender	Algorithm 2 Mean Adversary, Defender	p-value Adversary, Defender
MAVIPER	IVIPER	2	0.5275, *0.8450*	0.4211, 0.5787	0.3470, **0.0000**
		4	0.6494, *0.9112*	0.7191, 0.7843	0.4415, **0.0000**
		6	0.9656, *0.9399*	0.6717, 0.8460	**0.0000, 0.0000**
MAVIPER	Imitation DT	2	0.5275, *0.8450*	0.3710, 0.5787	0.0808, **0.0000**
		4	0.6494, *0.9112*	0.7512, 0.7003	0.1405, **0.0000**
		6	0.9656, *0.9399*	0.7761, 0.7833	**0.0117, 0.0000**
MAVIPER	Fitted Q-Iteration	2	0.5275, *0.8450*	0.1380, 0.1191	**0.0000, 0.0000**
		4	0.6494, *0.9112*	0.1406, 0.1204	**0.0000, 0.0000**
		6	0.9656, *0.9399*	0.1390, 0.1940	**0.0000, 0.0000**
IVIPER	Imitation DT	2	0.4211, 0.5787	0.3710, 0.5787	0.8567, **1.0000**
		4	0.7191, *0.7843*	0.7512, 0.7003	0.8978, **0.0016**
		6	0.6717, *0.8460*	0.7761, 0.7833	0.2850, **0.0119**
IVIPER	Fitted Q-Iteration	2	0.4211, *0.5787*	0.1380, 0.1191	**0.0004, 0.0000**
		4	0.7191, *0.7843*	0.1406, 0.1204	**0.0000, 0.0000**
		6	0.6717, *0.8460*	0.1390, 0.1940	**0.0000, 0.0000**
Imitation DT	Fitted Q-Iteration	2	0.3710, *0.5787*	0.1380, 0.1191	**0.0039, 0.0000**
		4	0.7512, *0.7003*	0.1406, 0.1204	**0.0000, 0.0000**
		6	0.7761, *0.7833*	0.1390, 0.1940	**0.0000, 0.0000**

depth of 4: $F(3, 36) = 76.9866$, $p = 0.0000$; maximum depth of 6: $F(3, 36) = 75.4581$, $p = 0.0000$). To determine the groups that contributed to this result, a post-hoc Tukey's HSD test for multiple comparisons with Bonferroni correction was conducted. This test showed that, for all maximum depths, the following pairs have significant differences: MAVIPER and Fitted Q-Iteration, IVIPER and Fitted Q-Iteration, and Imitation DT and Fitted Q-Iteration. For a maximum depth of 6, only IVIPER and Imitation DT did not exhibit significant differences. These results mean there is almost no difference between MAVIPER, IVIPER, and Imitation DT in the case of this adversary, so the correct strategy may be simple enough to capture with a less-sophisticated algorithm.

Now looking at the defenders, a one-way ANOVA was similarly performed. It revealed that there was a statistically significant difference in the individual performance ratio for the defenders between at least two groups for all depths (maximum depth of 2: $F(3, 36) = 76.2633$, $p = 0.0000$; maximum depth of 4: $F(3, 36) = 558.7447$, $p = 0.0000$; maximum depth of 6: $F(3, 36) = 786.663$, $p = 0.0000$). A post-hoc Tukey's HSD test for multiple comparisons with Bonferroni correction determined that MAVIPER defenders significantly outperform all other algorithms. This test further revealed that IVIPER defenders significantly outperform Imitation DT (on all depths except for 2) and Fitted Q-Iteration defenders. Table 5.1 shows the full results of these tests, where the defender performance is recorded on the right side of the three rightmost columns. Because MAVIPER significantly outperforms all other algorithms when coordination is needed, these results indicate that it promotes coordination between agents even in the single-agent training regime.

Figure 5.2c indicates that agents perform similarly on the cooperative navigation environment. These results are not unexpected because the original MADDPG paper mentions that this environment has a less stark contrast between success and failure (Lowe et al. 2017). For each maximum depth, a one-way ANOVA was conducted to compare the effect of the four different decision-tree training algorithms on the individual performance ratio for this environment (Table 5.2). This test revealed that there was a statistically significant difference in the individual performance ratio between at least two algorithms for all depths (maximum depth of 2: $F(3, 36) = 10.3421$, $p = 0.0000$; maximum depth of 4: $F(3, 36) = 16.3784$, $p = 0.0000$; maximum depth of of 6: $F = 41.4938$, $p = 0.0000$). A post-hoc Tukey's HSD test with

TABLE 5.2 Tukey's HSD Results Comparing the Average Individual Performance for Cooperative Navigation. The Highest-Performing, Statistically Significant Results for Each Tree Depth (and the Corresponding p-Value) Are in **Bold**. The α Level is 0.05

Algorithm 1	Algorithm 2	Depth	Algorithm 1 Mean	Algorithm 2 Mean	p-value
MAVIPER	IVIPER	2	**0.6830**	0.6470	**0.0378**
		4	**0.7596**	0.7052	**0.0036**
		6	0.7811	0.7677	0.7680
MAVIPER	Imitation DT	2	**0.6830**	0.6153	**0.0000**
		4	**0.7596**	0.7139	**0.0177**
		6	0.7811	0.7837	0.9975
MAVIPER	Fitted Q-Iteration	2	0.6830	0.6665	0.5741
		4	**0.7596**	0.6574	**0.0000**
		6	**0.7811**	0.6525	**0.0000**
IVIPER	Imitation DT	2	0.6470	0.6153	0.0804
		4	0.7052	0.7139	0.9318
		6	0.7677	0.7837	0.6562
IVIPER	Fitted Q-Iteration	2	0.6470	0.6665	0.4359
		4	0.7052	0.6574	0.0871
		6	**0.7677**	0.6525	**0.0000**
Imitation DT	Fitted Q-Iteration	2	0.6153	**0.6665**	**0.0016**
		4	**0.7139**	0.6574	**0.0025**
		6	**0.7837**	0.6525	**0.0000**

Bonferroni correction showed that MAVIPER significantly outperformed the other algorithms, with the exceptions of: IVIPER and Imitation DT at a maximum depth of 6, and Fitted Q-Iteration at a maximum depth of 2. Those two comparisons did not exhibit a statistically significant difference. Furthermore, IVIPER and Imitation DT did not have statistically significant differences for all maximum depths. Indeed, IVIPER only significantly outperformed Fitted Q-Iteration when the maximum depth is 6; their means were indistinguishable otherwise. These results indicate that MAVIPER tends to yield higher-performing individual agents than the other algorithms. In contrast, IVIPER is generally indistinguishable from the baselines.

Figures 5.2d and 5.2e indicate that both MAVIPER predators and prey generally outperform those trained by the other algorithms. Looking first at the predators, a one-way ANOVA was again performed. This test showed a statistically significant difference in mean individual performance ratio between at least two of the algorithms for each maximum depth (maximum depth of 2: $F(3, 36) = 10.7644$, $p = 0.0000$; maximum depth of 4: $F(3, 36) = 20.2408$, $p = 0.0000$; maximum depth of

TABLE 5.3 Tukey's HSD Results Comparing the Average Individual Performance for Predators and Prey in the Predator–Prey Environment. The Highest-Performing, Statistically Significant Results for Each Tree Depth (and the Corresponding p-Value) Are in **Bold**. To Further Distinguish the Results, the Best-Performing Predator Is Denoted in **Underline**, and the Best-Performing Prey Is Denoted in **Italic** (if the Results Are Statistically Significant). Results Are Presented as: Predator, Prey. The α Level Is 0.05

Algorithm 1	Algorithm 2	Depth	Algorithm 1 Mean Predator, Prey	Algorithm 2 Mean Predator, Prey	p-value Predator, Prey
MAVIPER	IVIPER	2	0.6013, *1.0261*	0.6265, 0.6828	0.7441, **0.0006**
		4	0.7261, 0.9191	0.6531, 0.8765	**0.0344**, 0.8403
		6	0.7679, *0.9420*	0.7211, 0.8076	0.6136, **0.0044**
MAVIPER	Imitation DT	2	0.6013, *1.0261*	0.5456, 0.6965	0.1314, **0.0009**
		4	0.7261, *0.9191*	0.6296, 0.5676	**0.0031, 0.0000**
		6	0.7679, *0.9420*	0.7010, 0.5748	0.3111, **0.0000**
MAVIPER	Fitted Q-Iteration	2	0.6013, *1.0261*	0.4976, 0.6404	**0.0010, 0.0001**
		4	0.7261, *0.9191*	0.5291, 0.6023	**0.0000, 0.0000**
		6	0.7679, *0.9420*	0.5435, 0.6055	**0.0000, 0.0000**
IVIPER	Imitation DT	2	0.6265, 0.6828	0.5456, 0.6965	**0.0127**, 0.9981
		4	0.6531, *0.8765*	0.6296, 0.5676	0.7945, **0.0000**
		6	0.7211, *0.8076*	0.7010, 0.5748	0.9519, **0.0000**
IVIPER	Fitted Q-Iteration	2	0.6265, 0.6828	0.4976, 0.6404	**0.0000**, 0.9486
		4	0.6531, *0.8765*	0.5291, 0.6023	**0.0001, 0.0000**
		6	0.7211, *0.8076*	0.5435, 0.6055	**0.0002, 0.0000**
Imitation DT	Fitted Q-Iteration	2	0.5456, 0.6965	0.4976, 0.6404	0.2344, 0.8907
		4	0.6296, 0.5676	0.5291, 0.6023	**0.0020**, 0.9055
		6	0.7010, 0.5748	0.5435, 0.6055	**0.0011**, 0.8372

6: $F(3, 36) = 13.0601$, $p = 0.0000$). As shown in Table 5.3 (left-hand side of the rightmost columns), a post-hoc Tukey's HSD test with Bonferroni correction revealed MAVIPER-trained predators only significantly differed from the IVIPER-trained and Imitation-DT-trained predators when the maximum depth is 4. Otherwise, their means did not exhibit significant differences. However, MAVIPER and IVIPER significantly outperformed Fitted Q- Iteration for all depths. IVIPER only significantly outperformed Imitation DT with maximum depth 2.

Looking now at the prey, a one-way ANOVA was similarly conducted. This test revealed a statistically significant difference in the mean individual performance ratio between at least two groups for all maximum depths (maximum depth of 2: $F(3, 36) = 10.2907$, $p = 0.0000$; maximum depth of 4: $F(3, 36) = 25.1552$, $p = 0.000$; maximum depth of 6: $F(3, 36) = 44.5994$, $p = 0.0000$). As shown in Table 5.3 (right-hand side of the results columns), a post-hoc Tukey's HSD test with Bonferroni correction determined that MAVIPER significantly outperforms all other algorithms, except for IVIPER with a maximum depth of 4. In this case, there is no statistically significant difference between their means. IVIPER also significantly outperforms Imitation DT and Fitted Q-Iteration, except when the maximum depth is 2. In this case, there is no statistically significant difference between their means. Taken together, these results indicate that MAVIPER enables the prey agents to better avoid capture compared to IVIPER and the baselines, and that IVIPER enables the prey agents to better avoid capture compared to the baselines.

In summary, MAVIPER training tends to lead to higher-performing individual agents, especially when those agents are part of a team. This result suggests that MAVIPER-trained agents exhibit improved performance due to better coordination with their team.

JOINT PERFORMANCE COMPARED TO EXPERTS

A crucial aspect of multi-agent environments is agent coordination, especially when agents are on the same team with shared goals. One metric for coordination is the performance of the decision-tree policies when all agents in a team adopt decision-tree policies compared with their expert policies, while other agents deploy their expert policies. Specifically, the joint performance ratio is:

$$\textit{Joint performance ratio} = E\left[U_Z^{\pi^*_{-Z}}\right] = \frac{U_Z(\hat{\pi}_Z, \pi^*_{-Z})}{U_Z(\pi^*)},$$

where $U_Z(\hat{\pi}_Z, \pi^*_{-Z})$ is the utility of team Z when using their decision-tree policies against the expert policies of the other agents $-Z$. This metric captures any performance degradation compared to the experts. These experiments test hypothesis **H2**.

Figure 5.3 shows the mean joint performance ratio for each team, averaged over all trials. Compared with Figure 5.2, Figure 5.3 highlights the performance degradation when moving from individual to joint performance. This outcome is expected: MADDPG policies can capture more nuanced behavior, so they are more readily able to compensate for deficiencies in their “partner” policies. Figure 5.3a shows that MAVIPER defenders achieve higher joint performance than defenders trained by IVIPER and the baselines in physical deception, indicating that it better captures the coordinated behavior necessary for success. IVIPER defenders also perform better than the baselines. In contrast, Fitted

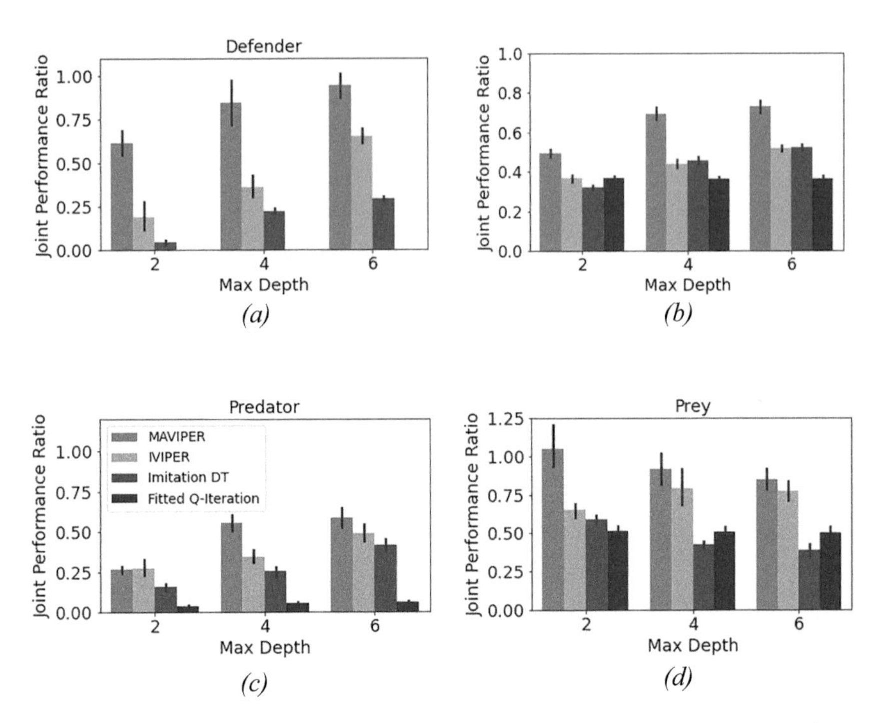

FIGURE 5.3 Joint performance ratio: relative performance when a team adopts their decision tree policies and all other agents use an expert policy. Higher is better. Error bars correspond to the 95% confidence interval. (First published in Milani et al. 2022 by Springer Nature. Reproduced with permission by Springer Nature.) *(a) Joint defender performance, Physical Deception. (b) Joint agent performance, Cooperative Navigation. (c) Joint predator performance, Predator–Prey. (d) Joint prey performance, Predator–Prey.*

Q-Iteration struggles to achieve coordinated behavior, despite obtaining non-zero success for individual agents. This algorithm likely struggles due to poor Q-value estimates.

A closer look into the performance of these algorithms revealed that there was a statistically significant difference in the joint performance ratio between at least two of the algorithms for each maximum depth (Table 5.4). This result was determined by a one-way ANOVA conducted for each maximum depth (maximum depth of 2: $F(3, 36) = 88.8662$, $p = 0.0000$; maximum depth of 4: $F(3, 36) = 83.3715$, $p = 0.0000$; maximum depth of 6: $F(3, 36) = 380.76$, $p = 0.0000$). A post-hoc Tukey's HSD test determined which algorithms are responsible for this difference. Critically, MAVIPER agents significantly outperformed all other agent types for all maximum depths. IVIPER agents also significantly outperformed the

TABLE 5.4 Tukey's HSD Results Comparing the Average Joint Performance for the Defenders in the Physical Deception Environment. The Highest-Performing, Statistically Significant Results for Each Comparison at Each Tree Depth (and the Corresponding p-Value) Are in **Bold**. The α Level Is 0.05

Algorithm 1	Algorithm 2	Depth	Algorithm 1 Mean	Algorithm 2 Mean	p-value
MAVIPER	IVIPER	2	**0.6150**	0.1879	**0.0000**
		4	**0.8454**	0.3621	**0.0000**
		6	**0.9450**	0.6548	**0.0000**
MAVIPER	Imitation DT	2	**0.6150**	0.0465	**0.0000**
		4	**0.8454**	0.2237	**0.0000**
		6	**0.9450**	0.2943	**0.0000**
MAVIPER	Fitted Q-Iteration	2	**0.6150**	0.0000	**0.0000**
		4	**0.8454**	0.0000	**0.0000**
		6	**0.9450**	0.0110	**0.0000**
IVIPER	Imitation DT	2	**0.1879**	0.0465	**0.0095**
		4	0.3621	0.2237	0.0773
		6	**0.6548**	0.2943	**0.0000**
IVIPER	Fitted Q-Iteration	2	**0.1879**	0.0000	**0.0004**
		4	**0.3621**	0.0000	**0.0000**
		6	**0.6548**	0.0110	**0.0000**
Imitation DT	Fitted Q-Iteration	2	0.0465	0.0000	0.6884
		4	**0.2237**	0.0000	**0.0015**
		6	**0.2943**	0.0110	**0.0000**

baselines for all maximum depths, except for Imitation DT when the maximum depth is 4. In this case, there was no statistically significant difference between the two algorithms. These results indicate that both MAVIPER and IVIPER achieve better coordinated performance than the baselines; however, MAVIPER achieves the highest joint performance and, therefore, produces the best agents for coordination.

The superior performance of MAVIPER in this environment is likely due to the defender agents correctly splitting their "attention" to induce the correct behavior of covering both targets. Figure 5.4 investigates this possibility by showing the normalized average feature importance of the decision-tree policies of depth 4 for both IVIPER and MAVIPER over 5 (out of 10) randomly selected trials. Each of the MAVIPER defenders (top) most commonly focuses on the attributes associated with one specific target: defender 1 focuses on target 2, and defender 2 focuses on target 1. In contrast, both IVIPER defenders (bottom) mostly focus on the attributes associated with the goal target. Not only does this overlap in feature space mean that defenders are unlikely to capture the correct

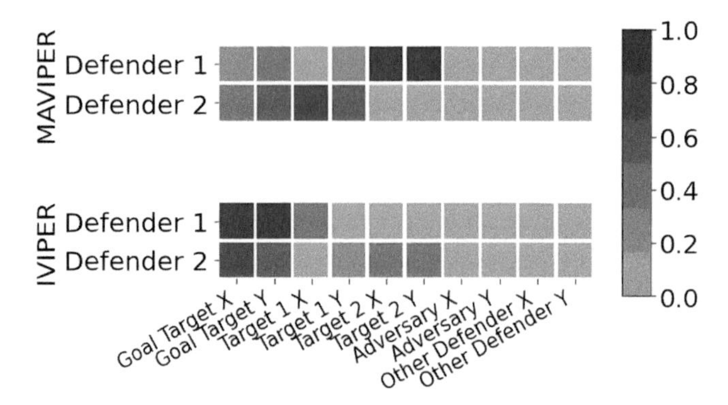

FIGURE 5.4 Feature importance of the two defenders trained by IVIPER and MAVIPER in the physical deception environment. Actual features are the relative positions of that agent and the labeled feature. Darker squares correspond to higher feature importance. MAVIPER defenders (top) frequently split importance across the two targets. In contrast, IVIPER defenders (bottom) most commonly focus on the same target (the goal target). To succeed in this environment, defenders must split their attention to the two different targets, not focusing on the goal target at the same time. (First published in Milani et al. 2022 by Springer Nature. Reproduced with permission by Springer Nature.)

covering behavior, but it also leaves them more vulnerable to an adversary because it is easier to infer the goal target.

MAVIPER also exhibits this better-coordinated behavior in the cooperative navigation environment. Indeed, Figure 5.3b shows that MAVIPER agents outperform all other algorithms in the cooperative navigation environment for all maximum depths. A one-way ANOVA for each maximum depth was conducted to compare the effect of the four different decision-tree training algorithms on the joint performance ratio for each maximum depth. This test revealed that there was a statistically significant difference in mean joint performance ratio for all maximum depths (maximum depth of 2: $F(3, 36) = 98.2534$, $p = 0.0000$; maximum depth of 4: $F(3, 36) = 166.533$, $p = 0.0000$; maximum depth of 6: $F(3, 36) = 202.3992$, $p = 0.0000$). Table 5.5 shows the results of a post-hoc Tukey's HSD test with Bonferroni correction applied to each maximum depth. Based on these results, MAVIPER significantly outperformed all other algorithms. IVIPER significantly outperformed the baselines for most conditions, with the exceptions of Imitation DT at a maximum depth of 4 and Fitted Q-Iteration at a maximum depth of 2. In those cases, the mean joint performance ratios were indistinguishable. Recall that, compared to physical deception, cooperative navigation introduces an

TABLE 5.5 Tukey's HSD Results Comparing the Average Joint Performance for the Agents in the Cooperative Navigation Environment. The Highest-Performing, Statistically Significant Results for Each Comparison at Each Tree Depth (and the Corresponding p-Value) Are in **Bold**. The α Level Is 0.05

Algorithm 1	Algorithm 2	Depth	Algorithm 1 Mean	Algorithm 2 Mean	p-value
MAVIPER	IVIPER	2	**0.4957**	0.3659	**0.0000**
		4	**0.6948**	0.4400	**0.0000**
		6	**0.7287**	0.5210	**0.0000**
MAVIPER	Imitation DT	2	**0.4957**	0.3223	**0.0000**
		4	**0.6948**	0.4598	**0.0000**
		6	**0.7287**	0.4598	**0.0000**
MAVIPER	Fitted Q-Iteration	2	**0.4957**	0.3705	**0.0000**
		4	**0.6948**	0.3653	**0.0000**
		6	**0.7287**	0.3657	**0.0000**
IVIPER	Imitation DT	2	**0.3659**	0.3223	**0.0012**
		4	0.4400	0.4598	0.5900
		6	**0.5210**	0.4598	**0.0016**
IVIPER	Fitted Q-Iteration	2	0.3659	0.3705	0.9737
		4	**0.4400**	0.3653	**0.0002**
		6	**0.5210**	0.3657	**0.0000**
Imitation DT	Fitted Q-Iteration	2	0.3223	**0.3705**	**0.0004**
		4	**0.4598**	0.3653	**0.0000**
		6	**0.4598**	0.3657	**0.0000**

additional agent with which the defenders must coordinate (and removes the adversary). The superior performance of MAVIPER agents indicates that MAVIPER better captures coordinated behavior, even as the complexity of the problem is increased by introducing another cooperating agent.

Figures 5.3c and 5.3d depicts the results for both teams in the predator–prey environment. These results do not offer a straightforward conclusion. To compare the effect of the choice of the decision-tree training algorithm on the joint performance ratio of the predators, a one-way ANOVA test for all maximum depths was conducted. This test revealed that there was a statistically significant difference in mean joint performance ratio between at least two groups for all maximum depths (maximum depth of 2: $F = 48.0960$, $p = 0.0000$; maximum depth of 4: $F = 140.8732$, $p = 0.0000$; maximum depth of 6: $F = 87.5597$, $p = 0.0000$). A post-hoc Tukey's HSD test with Bonferroni correction, applied for all maximum depths, found that MAVIPER-trained predator teams significantly outperform the two baselines.

However, predators trained by MAVIPER only significantly outperformed those trained by IVIPER when the maximum depth is 4; in all other settings, the two algorithms do not exhibit a statistically significant difference between means. IVIPER predators significantly outperform the baselines, except Imitation DT when the maximum depth is 6. In that case, the means are indistinguishable.

To compare the effect of the different decision tree training algorithms on the joint performance ratio of the prey, a one-way ANOVA was conducted for all maximum depths (Table 5.6). This test revealed that there was indeed a statistically significant difference in the mean joint performance ratio between at least two groups for all maximum depths (maximum depth of 2: $F = 35.08693$, $p = 0.0000$; maximum depth of 4: $F = 28.3989$, $p = 0.0000$; maximum depth of 6: $F = 60.6513$, $p = 0.0000$). A post-hoc Tukey's HSD test with Bonferroni correction, applied for all maximum depths, found that MAVIPER-trained prey significantly

TABLE 5.6 Tukey's HSD Results Comparing the Average Joint Performance for the Predators and Prey in the Predator–Prey Environment. The Highest-Performing, Statistically Significant Results for Each Comparison at Each Tree Depth (and the Corresponding p-Value) Are in **Bold**. To Further Distinguish the Results, the Best-Performing Predator is Denoted in **Underline**, and the Best-Performing Prey Is Denoted in **Italic** (if the Results Are Statistically Significant). Results Are Presented as: Predator, Prey. The α Level Is 0.05

Algorithm 1	Algorithm 2	Depth	Algorithm 1 Mean Predator, Prey	Algorithm 2 Mean Predator, Prey	p-value Predator, Prey
MAVIPER	IVIPER	2	0.2648, *1.0453*	0.2713, 0.6515	0.9917, **0.0000**
		4	0.5554, 0.9153	0.3455, 0.7932	**0.0000**, 0.2107
		6	0.5834, 0.8464	0.4906, 0.7750	0.0520, 0.2896
MAVIPER	Imitation DT	2	0.2648, *1.0453*	0.1566, 0.5904	**0.0002, 0.0000**
		4	0.5554, *0.9153*	0.2510, 0.4244	**0.0000, 0.0000**
		6	0.5834, *0.8464*	0.4182, 0.3878	**0.0002, 0.0000**
MAVIPER	Fitted Q-Iteration	2	0.2648, *1.0453*	0.0359, 0.5151	**0.0000, 0.0000**
		4	0.5554, *0.9153*	0.0536, 0.5115	**0.0000, 0.0000**
		6	0.5834, *0.8464*	0.0585, 0.5012	**0.0000, 0.0000**
IVIPER	Imitation DT	2	0.2713, 0.6515	0.1566, 0.5904	**0.0000**, 0.7031
		4	0.3455, *0.7932*	0.2510, 0.4244	**0.0029, 0.0000**
		6	0.4906, *0.7750*	0.4182, 0.3878	0.1771, **0.0000**
IVIPER	Fitted Q-Iteration	2	0.2713, 0.6515	0.0359, 0.5151	**0.0004**, 0.0921
		4	0.3455, *0.7932*	0.0536, 0.5115	**0.0000, 0.0003**
		6	0.4906, *0.7750*	0.0585, 0.5012	**0.0000, 0.0000**
Imitation DT	Fitted Q-Iteration	2	0.1566, 0.5904	0.0359, 0.5151	**0.0000**, 0.5475
		4	0.2510, 0.4244	0.0536, 0.5115	**0.0000**, 0.4963
		6	0.4182, 0.3878	0.0585, *0.5012*	**0.0000, 0.0339**

outperformed the two baselines for all maximum depths. However, there was no statistically significant difference in the mean joint performance ratio between MAVIPER and IVIPER for maximum depths of 4 and 6. Indeed, MAVIPER-trained prey only significantly outperformed IVIPER-trained prey when the maximum depth is 2. IVIPER prey significantly outperformed the baselines, except for Imitation DT and Fitted Q-Iteration when the maximum depth is 2. There was no statistically significant difference in joint performance ratio in that setting.

Unlike the other environments, there is a less stark difference between the performance of MAVIPER and IVIPER. The main difference between the algorithms is when they are compared to the baselines: MAVIPER predators and prey outperformed all baselines for all maximum depths; this was not the case for IVIPER, as there were a few instances where its mean joint performance ratio was statistically indistinguishable from the mean joint performance ratio of a baseline algorithm.

Taken together, the results on all three of these environments indicate that IVIPER and MAVIPER better capture the coordinated behavior necessary for a team to succeed, with MAVIPER significantly outperforming IVIPER in several environments. For all environments and all maximum depths, MAVIPER significantly outperforms the baselines when measuring the mean joint performance ratio. In general, these results support the hypothesis that MAVIPER-trained agents exhibit better-coordinated behavior than IVIPER and the baselines.

ROBUSTNESS TO DIFFERENT OPPONENTS

Given that the goal is deploying these policies in real-world scenarios with potentially many different types of adversaries, this section investigates the robustness of the decision tree policies. Specifically, this section investigates when a team using decision tree policies plays against a variety of opponents in mixed competitive-cooperative environments.

In this set of experiments, the decision trees are constrained to a maximum depth of 4. Given a decision tree policy profile $\hat{\pi}$, a team Z's performance against an alternative policy profile π' used by the opponents is:

$$\textit{Team performance against opponent } \pi' = U_Z(\hat{\pi}_Z, \pi'_{-Z}).$$

Each of the defender teams is evaluated against a broad set of opponent policies π': the policies generated by MAVIPER, IVIPER, Imitation DT,

TABLE 5.7 Average Robustness Results on Physical Deception and Predator–Prey. Reported Here Is the Mean Team Performance and Standard Deviation of the Decision Tree Policies for Each Team, Averaged Across a Variety of Opponent Policies. The Best-Performing Algorithm for Each Agent Type Is Shown in **Bold**. First Published in Milani et al. 2022 by Springer Nature. Reproduced with Permission by Springer Nature

Environment	Team	MAVIPER	IVIPER	Imitation DT	Fitted Q-Iteration
Physical deception	Defender	**0.77 ± 0.01**	0.33 ± 0.01	0.24 ± 0.03	0.00 ± 0.00
	Adversary	**0.42 ± 0.03**	**0.41 ± 0.03**	**0.42 ± 0.03**	0.07 ± 0.01
Predator–prey	Predator	**2.51 ± 0.72**	**1.98 ± 0.58**	1.14 ± 0.28	0.26 ± 0.11
	Prey	**1.76 ± 0.80**	**2.16 ± 1.24**	**2.36 ± 1.90**	1.11 ± 0.82

Fitted Q-Iteration, and MADDPG. Note that, in contrast to the other metrics, the scores reported here are the raw success ratios for physical deception and the number of collisions for predator–prey. These experiments test **H3**.

Table 5.7 shows the mean team performance averaged over all opponent policies for both environments. Bolded values correspond to the best-performing algorithm for each agent type. Only results where the means do not overlap when accounting for the standard deviation are bolded.

For physical deception, MAVIPER defenders outperform all other algorithms, with a gap of 0.44 between the team performance of agents trained by MAVIPER and the performance of agents trained by the next-best algorithm, IVIPER. This result indicates that MAVIPER learns coordinated defender policies that perform well against various adversaries. Also in the physical deception environment, MAVIPER, IVIPER, and Imitation DT adversaries perform similarly on average, with a similar standard deviation, which supports the idea that the adversary's desired behavior is simple enough to capture with a less-sophisticated algorithm. For predator–prey, MAVIPER predators outperform all other algorithms. Although Imitation DT prey exhibit the highest mean performance, it is indistinguishable from MAVIPER and IVIPER.

Tables 5.8 and 5.9 contain the full results for the two environments. For space reasons, only the averages are reported. Rather than presenting the full results, the best-performing agent of each type are labeled in either underline or italic. However, the best-performing agents of each type are only labeled in underline or italic if the 95% confidence intervals do not overlap. MADDPG is excluded from this calculation, since it is expected that MADDPG agents will outperform all other agent types.

TABLE 5.8 Robustness Results of Decision Tree Agents in the Physical Deception Environment. Results Are Presented as: Adversary Success Ratio, Defender Success Ratio. Higher Is Better. Excluding MADDPG, the Best-Performing Defender for Each Adversary Type Is in *Italic* and the Best-Performing Adversary for Each Defender Type Is in **Underline**. First Published in Milani et al. 2022 by Springer Nature. Reproduced With Permission by Springer Nature

			Defender		
Adversary	**MAVIPER**	**IVIPER**	**Imitation DT**	**Fitted Q-Iteration**	**MADDPG**
MAVIPER	0.42, *0.76*	0.45, 0.33	0.45, 0.23	0.37, 0.01	0.40, 0.93
IVIPER	0.39, *0.78*	0.45, 0.32	0.40, 0.23	0.38, 0.00	0.43, 0.92
Imitation DT	0.40, *0.79*	0.42, 0.34	0.46, 0.26	0.38, 0.01	0.46, 0.92
Fitted Q-Iteration	0.07, *0.77*	0.06, 0.33	0.07, 0.19	0.08, 0.00	0.08, 0.79
MADDPG	0.71, *0.76*	0.77, 0.32	0.77, 0.26	0.58, 0.00	0.62, 0.90

TABLE 5.9 Robustness Results of Decision Tree Agents in the Predator–Prey Environment. Results Are Presented as: Average Number of Collisions per Episode (Predator), Average Number of Collisions per Episode (Prey). These Values Are the Same, but They Are Duplicated to Show Which Algorithms Are the Best-Performing Ones for Both Types of Agents. Higher is Better for the Predator, and Lower is Better for the Prey. Excluding MADDPG, the Best-Performing Prey for Each Predator Type Is in **Italic** and the Best-Performing Predator for Each Prey Type Is in **Underline**. First Published in Milani et al. 2022 by Springer Nature. Reproduced With Permission by Springer Nature

			Prey		
Predator	**MAVIPER**	**IVIPER**	**Imitation DT**	**Fitted Q-Iteration**	**MADDPG**
MAVIPER	2.28, *2.28*	3.49, 3.49	2.41, 2.41	3.01, 3.01	1.37, 1.37
IVIPER	1.95, *1.95*	2.46, 2.46	2.17, 2.17	2.44, 2.44	0.88, 0.88
Imitation DT	1.32, 1.32	1.17, *1.17*	1.18, *1.18*	1.40, 1.40	0.61, 0.61
Fitted Q-Iteration	0.46, 0.46	0.30, 0.30	0.24, 0.24	0.18, *0.18*	0.14, 0.14
MADDPG	2.78, *2.78*	3.36, 3.36	5.82, 5.82	4.98, 4.98	2.54, 2.54

Table 5.8 shows the results for the physical deception environment. MAVIPER defenders are more robust than all agents, excluding MADDPG, to different types of adversaries. This result can be easily seen by fixing the adversary row and comparing the success ratios of the different defenders in each column. In contrast, MAVIPER, IVIPER, and Imitation DT adversaries perform similarly. This result can be easily seen by fixing the defender column and comparing the success ratios of the different adversaries in each row. For simplicity, only the best-performing adversaries are noted in bold, since the 95% confidence intervals tend to overlap for most adversary types. MAVIPER adversaries perform best against MAVIPER defenders; MAVIPER and IVIPER adversaries perform

best against IVIPER defenders; Imitation DT adversaries perform best against Imitation DT and MADDPG defenders; and MAVIPER, IVIPER, and Imitation DT adversaries perform best against Fitted Q-Iteration defenders. This result aligns with the previous performance results, where MAVIPER, IVIPER, and Imitation DT adversaries performed similarly against MADDPG agents.

Table 5.9 shows the results for the predator–prey environment. MAVIPER predators are strictly more robust than all other agents, excluding MADDPG, to different types of prey. This result can be easily seen by fixing the prey column and comparing the average number of collisions per episode in each row. Recall that, for predators, a higher value is better. Furthermore, MAVIPER prey are generally either the most robust or the second-most robust to different types of predators. This result can be seen by fixing the predator row and comparing the average number of collisions per episode in each column. Recall that, for the predators, a higher value is better. In this environment, predator coordination is more critical because predators must work together to strategically catch the prey. On the other hand, the prey does not require much coordination. This lack of coordination explains the robustness of the Imitation DT prey by imitating the actions of the corresponding single-agent expert.

Taken together, these results indicate that MAVIPER-trained agents are generally more robust than agents trained with the other decision tree learning algorithms. These results indicate that MAVIPER-trained agents may be better suited for deployment in real-world scenarios where one expects to encounter a variety of attacker types, such as cybersecurity. Further work is needed to investigate the robustness of these policies in more realistic domains.

ABLATION STUDY OF MAVIPER

Given the improved performance of MAVIPER compared to IVIPER, it is important to understand which changes contribute to these differences. Recall the differences between MAVIPER and IVIPER. First, MAVIPER utilizes the predicted behavior of the anticipated decision trees of the other agents to grow each agent's tree. In contrast, IVIPER trains each agent's decision tree policy without utilizing these predictions. Second, the resampling probability of MAVIPER incorporates the average Q-values over all actions for the other agents. In contrast, IVIPER only considers the optimal actions of the other agents.

To investigate the contribution of these changes to the performance of MAVIPER, this section analyzes an ablation study with a maximum tree depth of 4 on the physical deception environment. In this setting, MAVIPER and IVIPER defenders achieve similar individual performance, but MAVIPER defenders outperform IVIPER defenders when measuring joint performance. Figure 5.5 shows the mean independent and joint performance ratios for each defender team, comparing MAVIPER and IVIPER to two variants of MAVIPER without one of the two critical changes.

This section first investigates the differences in the individual performance ratios for the adversaries. A one-way ANOVA was conducted to determine the effect of the algorithmic changes on the individual performance ratio. This test revealed that there was not a statistically significant difference between the group means ($F(3, 36) = 0.6314$, $p = 0.5995$). Therefore, all algorithms are effectively equivalent for the adversaries.

The next investigation is into the differences in the individual performance ratios for the defenders. To determine the effect of the algorithmic changes on the individual performance ratio, a one-way ANOVA test was conducted. This test revealed that there was a statistically significant difference between at least two groups ($F(3, 36) = 5.7287$, $p = 0.0026$). A post-hoc Tukey's HSD test with Bonferroni correction revealed that the mean value of individual performance ratios was significantly different between MAVIPER and MAVIPER with IVIPER resampling, referred to as MAVIPER (IVIPER Resampling) ($p = 0.0128$), and MAVIPER and IVIPER ($p = 0.0025$).

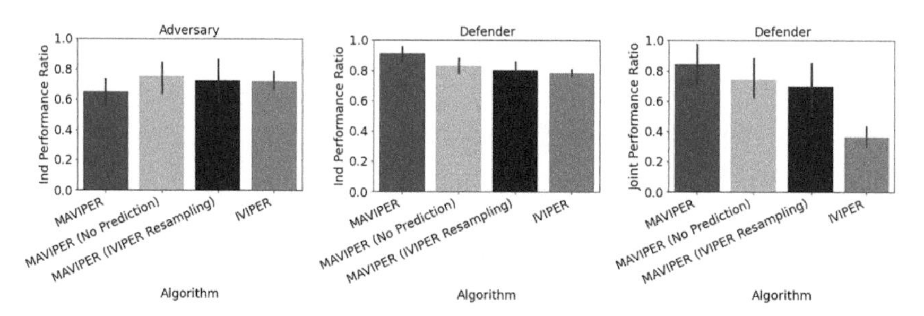

FIGURE 5.5 Ablation study for MAVIPER for a maximum depth of 4. MAVIPER (No prediction) does not utilize the predicted behavior of the other agents' anticipated decision trees to grow each agent's tree. MAVIPER (IVIPER Resampling) uses the same resampling method as IVIPER. (First published in Milani et al. 2022 by Springer Nature. Reproduced with permission by Springer Nature.)

In both of these cases, MAVIPER has a higher mean. All other pairs had p-values greater than the chosen α, so their differences in means were not statistically significant. As a result, the most significant algorithmic change for this metric seems to be the prediction module.

The final investigation is into the differences in the joint performance ratios for the defender. A one-way ANOVA was conducted to determine the effect of the algorithmic changes on the joint performance ratio. This test revealed that there was a statistically significant difference between at least two groups ($F(3,\ 36) = 10.6768,\ p = 0.0000$). A post-hoc Tukey's HSD test with Bonferroni correction revealed that the mean value of joint performance ratios was significantly different between the following pairs MAVIPER and IVIPER ($p = 0.0000$), MAVIPER with no prediction module, referred to as MAVIPER (No Prediction), and IVIPER ($p = 0.0010$), and MAVIPER (IVIPER Resampling) and IVIPER ($p = 0.0039$). In all cases, the first algorithm in the comparison has a higher mean. All other pairs had differences in means that were not statistically significant. This means that both ablated changes contribute to the improvement over IVIPER for this metric.

RELATED WORK

Most work on interpretable reinforcement learning is in the single-agent setting (Milani et al. 2022). Some work directly learns decision tree policies by augmenting the environment to include actions corresponding to splits of a decision tree and recording the outcomes in the state (Topin et al. 2021). Although it enables training with any function approximator during training, this transformation renders the learning problem more complex, especially in multi-agent settings. Other publications present custom algorithms that directly learn decision tree policies (McCallum 1997; Uther & Veloso 2000; Ernst et al. 2005), but not for interpretability. These algorithms cannot use a high-performing neural network to guide training.

Despite increased interest in interpretable single-agent reinforcement learning, there are few research efforts in interpretable multi-agent reinforcement learning. The majority of work uses attention (Iqbal & Sha 2019; Li, Jin, & Wang 2019; Motokawa & Sugawara 2021) to select and focus on critical factors that impact agents' decision making. Other work generates verbal explanations with predefined rules (Wang et al. 2020) or Shapley values (Heuillet, Couthouis, & Díaz-Rodríguez 2022). The most similar line of work (Kazhdan, Shams, & Liò 2020) to IVIPER and

MAVIPER constructs argument preference graphs, not decision tree policies, given manually provided arguments. Since the publication of Milani et al. (2022), a couple more relevant works have emerged. Grupen et al. (2022) propose to utilize concept bottlenecks in multi-agent reinforcement learning to understand emergent behavior. Guo et al. (2022) demonstrates how explanations in the form of decision tree policies can be used as a knowledge transfer technique in multi-agent reinforcement learning.

CONCLUSION

This chapter discussed IVIPER and MAVIPER, the first algorithms that extract interpretable decision tree policies for multi-agent reinforcement learning. This chapter presented results from evaluating these algorithms in cooperative and mixed competitive-cooperative environments. The results demonstrated that IVIPER and MAVIPER achieve near-expert performance: a single agent trained with these algorithms can recover at least 75% of expert performance in most environment settings – even with a small maximum depth – and over 90% in some. Furthermore, the results empirically validated that MAVIPER effectively captures coordinated behavior by showing that teams of MAVIPER-trained agents recover more of the expert performance on nearly all environments and maximum depths compared to the other algorithms. The chapter further showed that MAVIPER generally produces more robust agents than the other learning algorithms. Future work should seek to validate the effectiveness of these policies in assisting people with performing multi-agent tasks through extensive, task-grounded user studies.

ACKNOWLEDGMENTS

This material is based upon work supported by the Department of Defense (DoD) through the National Defense Science & Engineering Graduate (NDSEG) Fellowship Program. This research was sponsored by the U.S. Army Combat Capabilities Development Command Army Research Laboratory and was accomplished under Cooperative Agreement Number W911NF-13-2-0045 (ARL Cyber Security CRA). This work was supported in part by NSF grant IIS-2046640 (CAREER). Any opinions, findings, and conclusions or recommendations expressed in this material are those of the author(s) and do not reflect the views of the funding agencies or government agencies. The U.S. government is authorized to reproduce and distribute reprints for government purposes notwithstanding any copyright notation here on.

REFERENCES

Abbeel, P., & Ng, A. (2004). Apprenticeship learning via inverse reinforcement learning. In *Proceedings of the International Conference on Machine Learning.*

Bastani, O., Pu, Y., & Solar-Lezama, A. (2018). Verifiable reinforcement learning via pol-icy extraction. arXiv preprint arXiv:1805.08328.

Berner, C., Brockman, G., Chan, B., Cheung, V., Dębiak, P., Dennison, C. others. (2019). Dota 2 with large scale deep reinforcement learning. arXiv preprint arXiv:1912.06680.

Breiman, L., Friedman, J. H., Olshen, R. A., & Stone, C. J. (2017). *Classification and regression trees.* Routledge.

Buciluă, C., Caruana, R., & Niculescu-Mizil, A. (2006). Model compression. In *Proceedings of the International Conference on Knowledge Discovery and Data Mining.*

Chen, Z., Silvestri, F., Tolomei, G., Zhu, H., Wang, J., & Ahn, H. (2021). ReLACE: Reinforcement Learning Agent for Counterfactual Explanations of Arbitrary Predictive Models. arXiv preprint arXiv:2110.11960.

Ernst, D., Geurts, P., & Wehenkel, L. (2005). Tree-based batch mode reinforcement learning. *Journal of Machine Learning Research*, 6, 503–556.

Foerster, J., Farquhar, G., Afouras, T., Nardelli, N., & Whiteson, S. (2018). Counterfactual multi-agent policy gradients. In *Proceedings of the AAAI Conference on Artificial Intelligence.*

Grupen, N., Jaques, N., Kim, B., & Omidshafiei, S. (2022). Concept-based Understanding of Emergent Multi-Agent Behavior. In *Deep Reinforcement Learning Workshop NeurIPS 2022.*

Guo, Y., Campbell, J., Stepputtis, S., Li, R., Hughes, D., Fang, F., & Sycara, K. (2022). Explainable Action Advising for Multi-Agent Reinforcement Learning. *arXiv preprint arXiv:2211.07882.*

Hancock, T., Jiang, T., Li, M., & Tromp, J. (1996). Lower bounds on learning decision lists and trees. *Information and Computation, 126*(2), 114–122.

Heuillet, A., Couthouis, F., & Díaz-Rodríguez, N. (2022). Collective explainable AI: Explaining cooperative strategies and agent contribution in multiagent reinforcement learning with shapley values. *IEEE Computational Intelligence Magazine, 1*(71), 59–71.

Hinton, G., Vinyals, O., & Dean, J. (2015). Distilling the knowledge in a neural network. arXiv preprint arXiv:1503.02531.

Iqbal, S., & Sha, F. (2019). Actor-attention-critic for multi-agent reinforcement learning. In *Proceedings of the International Conference on Machine Learning.*

Kazhdan, D., Shams, Z., & Liò, P. (2020). MARLeME: A multi-agent reinforcement learning model extraction library. In *Proceedings of the International Joint Conference on Neural Networks.*

Li, S., Wu, Y., Cui, X., Dong, H., Fang, F., & Russell, S. (2019). Robust multi-agent rein-forcement learning via minimax deep deterministic policy gradient. In *Proceedings of the AAAI Conference on Artificial Intelligence.*

Li, W., Jin, B., & Wang, X. (2019). SparseMAAC: Sparse Attention for Multi-agent Reinforcement Learning. In *Proceedings of the International Conference on Database Systems for Advanced Applications.*

Littman, M. (1994). Markov games as a framework for multi-agent reinforcement learning. In *Machine Learning.*

Lowe, R., Wu, Y., Tamar, A., Harb, J., Abbeel, P., & Mordatch, I. (2017). Multi-agent actor-critic for mixed cooperative-competitive environments. arXiv preprint arXiv:1706.02275.

Luss, R., Dhurandhar, A., & Liu, M. (2022). Local Explanations for Reinforcement Learning. arXiv preprint arXiv:2202.03597.

Matignon, L., Laurent, G. J., & Le Fort-Piat, N. (2012). Independent reinforcement learners in cooperative Markov games: a survey regarding coordination problems. *The Knowledge Engineering Review*, 27(1), 1–31.

McCallum, R. (1997). *Reinforcement learning with selective perception and hidden state.* PhD Thesis, University of Rochester, Department of Computer Science.

Meng, Z., Wang, M., Bai, J., Xu, M., Mao, H., & Hu, H. (2020). Interpreting deep learning-based networking systems. In *Proceedings of the Annual Conference of the ACM Special Interest Group on Data Communication on the Applications, Technologies, Architectures, and Protocols for Computer Communication*, 154–171.

Milani, S., Topin, N., Veloso, M., & Fang, F. (2022). A Survey of Explainable Reinforcement Learning. arXiv preprint arXiv:2202.08434.

Milani, S., Zhang, Z., Topin, N., Shi, Z. R., Kamhoua, C., Papalexakis, E. E., & Fang, F. (2022). MAVIPER: Learning Decision Tree Policies for Interpretable Multi-Agent Reinforcement Learning. In *Proceedings of the European Conference on Machine Learning and Principles and Practice of Knowledge Discovery in Databases.*

Motokawa, Y., & Sugawara, T. (2021). MAT-DQN: Toward Interpretable Multi-Agent Deep Reinforcement Learning for Coordinated Activities. In *International Conference on Artificial Neural Networks*, 556–567.

Oliehoek, F., Spaan, M., & Vlassis, N. (2008). Optimal and approximate Q-value functions for decentralized POMDPs. *Journal of Artificial Intelligence Research, 32.*

Paszke, A., Gross, S., Chintala, S., Chanan, G., Yang, E., DeVito, Z., & others. (2017). Automatic differentiation in pytorch. In: NIPS 2017 Workshop Autodiff.

Quinlan, J. (1986). Induction of decision trees. *Machine Learning, 11*, 81–106.

Rashid, T., Samvelyan, M., Schroeder, C., Farquhar, G., Foerster, J., & Whiteson, S. (2018). Qmix: Monotonic value function factorisation for deep multi-agent reinforcement learning. In *Proceedings of the International Conference on Machine Learning.*

Ross, S., Gordon, G., & Bagnell, D. (2011). A reduction of imitation learning and structured prediction to no-regret online learning. In *Proceedings of the International Conference on Artificial Intelligence and Statistics.*

Shapley, L. (1953). Stochastic games. *Proceedings of the National Academy of Sciences, 39*, 10.

Son, K., Kim, D., Kang, W., Hostallero, D., & Yi, Y. (2019). Qtran: Learning to factorize with transformation for cooperative multi-agent reinforcement learning. arXiv preprint arXiv:1905.05408.

Sunehag, P., Lever, G., Gruslys, A., Czarnecki, W., Zambaldi, V., Jaderberg, M., & others. (2017). Value-decomposition networks for cooperative multi-agent reinforcement learning. arXiv preprint arXiv:1706.05296.

Topin, N., Milani, S., Fang, F., & Veloso, M. (2021). Iterative Bounding MDPs: Learning Interpretable Policies via Non-Interpretable Methods. In *Proceedings of the AAAI Conference on Artificial Intelligence.*

Uther, W., & Veloso, M. (2000). The lumberjack algorithm for learning linked decision forests. In *International Symposium on Abstraction, Reformulation, and Approximation.*

Wang, X., Li, H., Liu, R., Zhang, H., Lewis, M., & Sycara, K. (2020). Explanation of Reinforcement Learning Model in Dynamic Multi-Agent System. arXiv preprint arXiv:2008.01508.

Yu, C., Velu, A., Vinitsky, E., Wang, Y., Bayen, A., & Wu, Y. (2021). The surprising effectiveness of mappo in cooperative, multi-agent games. arXiv preprint arXiv:2103.01955.

CHAPTER 6

Towards the Automatic Synthesis of Interpretable Chess Tactics

Abhijeet Krishnan and Chris Martens
North Carolina State University, Raleigh, NC

INTRODUCTION

Recent advancements in reinforcement learning (RL) have produced agents capable of competing with and even outperforming the best human experts at various games like chess (Silver et al. 2018), Go (Silver et al. 2016), Shogi (Li et al. 2020), Mahjong (Silver et al. 2018), StarCraft II (Vinyals et al. 2019), and Dota 2 (Berner et al. 2019). These agents do not simply take advantage of faster reaction and calculation abilities, but are actually employing new, better strategies that lead to more victories. Borrowing from Jeanette Wing's definition of computational thinking (Wing 2008), these agents have better abstractions than human experts for the games they are trained to play.

Despite the existence of such agents in various competitive games, we still see human competition continue to thrive, with these agents leading to new ways of thinking and a re-evaluation of long-held beliefs about the game. These discoveries have, so far, involved manual or engine-assisted analysis of the games played by the agents (Sadler & Regan 2019; Zhou 2018). If the agents could themselves explain their strategies and decision making to human players, we posit that it would help improve their play.

DOI: 10.1201/9781003355281-6

Such chess-playing agents (chess engines) are used extensively in game analysis (Smith 2004; Tukmakov 2020) and tournament preparation (Andrei 2021). Expert chess players utilize engine move suggestions and evaluations to analyze new lines to play (PTI 2016). Most current engines use a neural network model with many thousands of parameters trained using deep reinforcement learning (DRL) in conjunction with a search algorithm to produce game moves. Examples include Monte Carlo Tree Search in AlphaZero (Silver et al. 2016), Predictor+Upper Confidence Bound tree search in Leela Chess Zero (Pascutto and Linscott 2019), or alpha-beta pruning in Stockfish 14 (Romstad, Costalba, & Kiiski 2021). However, this differs from how human chess players employ pattern recognition to produce moves (de Groot 1946; Connors, Burns, & Campitelli 2011).

Current research in the newly emerging field of explainable RL (XRL) attempts to develop methods to help humans understand RL agent decisions. Multiple techniques like t-SNE (Moore & Stamper 2019), trajectory clustering (Osborn, Samuel, & Mateas 2018), and heatmaps (Broll et al. 2019) have been applied to visualize agent behavior in games. Symbolic policies have been investigated as interpretable representations of neural network policies learned via DRL. They have been learned directly from reward signals (Trivedi et al. 2021; Landajuela et al. 2021), as surrogate models for more complex policies (Verma et al. 2018) or from input/output pairs (Derner, Kubalík, & Babuška 2018). However, most research in this area learns policies for optimal control in continuous environments, with discrete game environments like chess receiving little attention.

In this chapter, we propose a framework to learn a symbolic sub-policy model for chess. We describe our sub-policy as being a collection of first-order logic rules that model chess tactics. We use patterns learned by an existing inductive logic programming (ILP) system called PAL (Patterns and Learning) (Morales 1992) to derive these tactics. We contribute a divergence metric to evaluate our model of a tactic using the move evaluation capabilities of a chess engine. We present an evaluation of a set of tactics obtained from PAL against a random baseline using our metrics. Finally, we propose a computational evaluation of this approach by augmenting a chess engine with the synthesized tactics. We conclude with a discussion on the limitations of this approach, along with future work.

RELATED WORK

Strategy Synthesis

A number of research efforts attempt to learn rule-based agents using evolutionary approaches to play role-playing games like *Neverwinter Nights* (Spronck, Sprinkhuizen-Kuyper, & Postma 2004), board games like Checkers and Reversi (Benbassat & Sipper 2011), cooperative games like Hanabi (Canaan et al. 2018), platforms like Mario (de Freitas, de Souza, & Bernardino 2018), and real-time strategy games like μRTS (Mariño et al. 2021). Partially applicable strategies for puzzle games have been learned using constraint satisfaction (Butler, Torlak, & Popovic 2017). Our model for chess tactics is learned using ILP, and incorporates domain knowledge of the concept of a tactic in order to improve interpretability.

Explainable RL

Attempts to make RL agent policies amenable to human interpretation have been pursued in the XRL field. Puiutta and Veith (2020) provide a survey of recent XRL methods. An interpretability technique that has received some attention is that of training an inherently interpretable *surrogate model* that matches the performance of the original agent. Options for this surrogate model that have been investigated include decision trees (Bastani, Pu, & Solar-Lezama 2018; Coppens et al. 2019; Sieusahai and Guzdial 2021) and programmatic policies (Verma et al. 2018; Trivedi et al. 2021). Our proposed sub-policy model is only partially applicable, and attempts to improve interpretability for chess by incorporating domain knowledge of how chess tactics are structured.

Chess Pattern Learning

Chess has been called the *drosophila*[1] of artificial intelligence (McCarthy 1990). It has been a mainstay of AI research from the invention of the digital computer (Shannon 1950) to the neural network revolution (Silver et al. 2018). Given the depth of experimentation with AI techniques for chess, it is not surprising that the idea of using patterns to guide a computer to play chess is not new. Patterns have been used to suggest moves and guide playing strategies in middle-game positions (Berliner 1975; Pitrat 1977; Wilkins 1979) and endgames (Huberman 1968; Bramer 1977; Bratko 1982). Levinson and Snyder (1991) used weighted patterns in their Morph system as an evaluation function to guide playing strategy. Recent work has attempted to directly probe neural network engines to test for the presence of human concepts (McGrath et al. 2021). Morales (1992) developed the PAL system to learn first-order patterns in chess using ILP. We build upon this work by taking advantage of modern chess engines to serve as the reference evaluation function to select learned patterns instead of hand-crafted heuristics.

BACKGROUND

Inductive Logic Programming

Inductive logic programming (ILP) is a form of symbolic machine learning where the goal is to induce a hypothesis (a set of logical rules) that generalizes given training examples (Cropper & Dumančić 2020). It can learn human-readable hypotheses from smaller amounts of data than neural network models.

An ILP problem is specified by three sets of Horn clauses—*B;* the background knowledge, E^+, the set of positive examples of the concept; and E^-, the set of negative examples of the concept. The ILP problem is to induce a hypothesis H that, in combination with the background knowledge, entails all the positive examples and none of the negative examples. Formally, this can be written as:

$$\forall\, e \in E^+,\ H \cup B \models e \quad (\text{i.e.},\ H \ \ is\ \ complete)$$
$$\forall\, e \in E^-,\ H \cup B \not\models e \quad (\text{i.e.},\ H \ \ is\ \ consistent)$$

To make the ILP problem more concrete, we provide a toy example below.

E^+ and E^- contain positive and negative examples of the target knight_move relation, respectively. *B* contains background knowledge (i.e., clauses that might be useful in inducing a hypothesis for knight_move).

$$E^+ = \{knight\_move(d4,\ c6).\ \ knight\_move(d4,\ e6).$$
$$knight\_move(d4,\ b5).\ \ knight\_move(d4, f5).\ \}$$
$$E^- = \{knight\_move(d4,\ d5).\ \ knight\_move(d4,\ b6).$$
$$knight\_move(d4,\ e1).\ \ knight\_move(d4,\ h7).\ \}$$
$$B = \{l\_move(d4,\ c6).\ \ l\_move(d4,\ e6).\ \ l\_move(d4,\ b5).$$
$$l\_move(d4, f5).\ \}$$

From this information, we could induce a hypothesis for knight_move as
knight_move(From,To):– l_move(From,To).

PAL System

The PAL (patterns and learning) system was introduced by Morales (1992). It attempts to use ILP to synthesize patterns for chess play, which are expressed using a subset of Horn clause logic. It contributes a predicate vocabulary for expressing these patterns and chess positions as Horn clauses. The pattern-learning problem is framed as an ILP problem, for which a heuristically constrained version of the *rlgg* (relative least general generalization) algorithm is used to induce plausible hypotheses. Patterns learned can be *static* and not involve any piece movement, or be *dynamic* and describe multi-move tactics. We expand upon how the PAL system formally defines and synthesizes these chess patterns.

Pattern Formalism

A pattern in PAL is formally defined as a non-recursive Horn clause of the form

$$\text{Head}: -D_1, D_2, \cdots, D_n, F_1, F_2, \cdots, F_m$$

where:

- Head is the head of the pattern definition
- The D_i are "input" predicates used to describe the position and represent pieces involved in the pattern
- The F_j are instances of definitions that are either provided as background knowledge or learned by PAL, and represent the conditions (relations between pieces and places) to be satisfied by the pattern.

An example of a *checking move* pattern, where a move that puts the opponent king in check is suggested, is reproduced from Morales (1992) in Figure 6.1. A key predicate is make_move, which determines whether a pattern is static or dynamic. The *contents* predicates are used to describe the position on the board. The remaining predicate definitions are provided as background knowledge.

```
can_check(S1,P1,(X1,Y1),S2,king,(X2,Y2),(X3,Y3),Pos1) :-
        contents(S1,P1,(X1,Y1),Pos1),
        contents(S2,king,(X2,Y2),Pos1),
        other_side(S1,S2),
        ¬in_check(S2,(X2,Y2),P1,(X1,Y1),Pos1),
        make_move(S1,P1,(X1,Y1),(X3,Y3),Pos1,Pos2),
        in_check(S2,(X2,Y2),P1,(X3,Y3),Pos2).
```

FIGURE 6.1 A PAL rule for the can_check pattern. A piece (P1) belonging to the side S1 can check the opponent's (S2) King after moving to (X3,Y3).

Pattern Synthesis

The input to the PAL generalization algorithm is a set of pattern definitions (both predefined and learned) along with a description of a chess position (as ground unit clauses). The algorithm extends Buntine's (1988) method for constructing the *rlgg* of two clauses to multiple clauses. It uses the following constraints and heuristics to limit hypothesis size and increase the algorithm's generalization steps:

- Disallowing variables in the head or body of a rule that are not *connected* to a literal (i.e., not equal to a variable of that literal)
- Labeling constants occurring in the ground literals of a rule body to make patterns piece-invariant
- Restricting the legal moves from a position to be only those that introduce a new predicate name or remove an existing predicate name

PAL uses an automatic example generator to manually guide the generalization algorithm towards learning desired concepts. Given an example of the target concept, the generator *perturbs* the example to create a new example for which a classification label must be provided. To restrict the example space searched, the automatic example generator attempts to generate examples which specialize the current hypothesis in case of a prior positive example, or generalize it in case of a prior negative example. We refer interested readers to the original thesis for further details.

METHODOLOGY

Chess Tactic Model

We conceptualize our sub-policy model as a *chess tactic*. Formally, we define a tactic as a first-order logic rule that can bind to a chess position. A position is expressed in first-order logic using an appropriate predicate vocabulary. If a tactic binds to (matches) a particular position, it suggests a move (or moves) to be played. The moves suggested must be legal in the given position. This is described in Figure 6.2 as a Prolog pseudo-definition.

A single tactic, or even a set of tactics, does not represent a complete policy for playing chess. This is because we might encounter a position for which no tactic matches. In this case, our model cannot make a move. There might also be positions to which multiple tactics apply, in which case an arbitration process for selecting a single move among the various suggestions is not obvious.

Tactic Utility Metrics

We introduce two metrics, *coverage* and *divergence*, to measure the utility of a learned tactic.

Coverage

A tactic t's coverage for a set of positions P is calculated as:

$$Coverage_t = \frac{|P_{match}|}{|P|}$$

where a position $p \in P_{\text{match}}$ if there is a binding assignment of the variables in the rule head of the tactic t to the position p.

Divergence

To measure the quality of moves suggested by a tactic, we extend a metric previously used to analyze world chess champions (Guid & Bratko 2006;

```
tactic(Position) :-
  matches(Position), !,
  suggested(Move1,Move2,···,MoveN),
  legal(Position,Move1),
  legal(Position,Move2),
  ⋮
  legal(Position,MoveN).
```

FIGURE 6.2 A Prolog pseudo-definition for a tactic. “!” is the Prolog cut operator.

2011; Romero 2019) to multiple moves using *discounted cumulative gain* (DCG) (Järvelin & Kekäläinen 2002). A move's *error* in a position p is measured by comparing it to the best move suggested by the engine in that position. This comparison is done quantitatively by using the engine's move evaluation function $eval(\cdot,p)$. In case an engine evaluates a position to be a 'Mate in X' rather than a centipawn score (a commonly used metric in computer chess to evaluate a position; defined as 1/100ths of the value of a pawn), we assign an arbitrary large value to the evaluation.

$$\text{Error}(move, p) = |eval(move_{\text{engine}}, p) - eval(move, p)|$$

Since a tactic might suggest multiple moves, we propose the use of DCG as a metric to compare ranked move suggestion lists. Assuming the list of suggestions output by a tactic to be in ranked order, we obtain a list of best moves from the engine of similar length as the suggestions, and compare the two using DCG. Thus, the final divergence metric for a tactic t over a set of positions P is:

$$Divergence_t = \frac{1}{|P_{match}|} \sum_{p \in P_{match}} \sum_{i=1}^{|M_t|} \frac{Error(m_i, p)}{log_2(1 + i)}$$

where M_t is the ranked list of move suggestions output by a tactic, and m_i is the ith move in M_t. The divergence of a tactic (to the reference engine) is low and close to 0 when its suggestions are similar in evaluation to the engine's best moves, and takes on large values when it differs substantially.

Implementation using PAL

We use the PAL system to synthesize tactics. We select seven patterns that PAL was shown to learn, and modify them to output a move suggestion. These patterns and their verbal definitions are listed in Table 6.1. All patterns learned other than pin are one-ply *dynamic* patterns, which means they include a single make_move predicate in the rule body looking ahead one move. We modify these patterns to introduce a suggestion predicate with the same variables as make_move. For pin, which is a static pattern as learned by PAL, we convert it into a dynamic pattern as shown in Figure 6.3 and introduce the suggestion predicate in the same way.

TABLE 6.1 Patterns Learned by the PAL System That Are Used to Create Tactics

Pattern	Definition
can_threat	A piece (P1) can threaten another piece (P2) after making a move to (X3,Y3)
can_fork	A piece (P1) can produce a fork to the opponent's King and another piece (P3) after making a move to (X4,Y4)
can_check	A piece (P1) can check the opponent's King after moving to (X3,Y3)
discovered_check	A check by piece (P2) can be "discovered" after moving another piece (P1) to (X4,Y4)
discovered_threat	A piece (P1) can threaten an opponent's piece (P3) after moving another piece (P2) to (X4,Y4)
skewer	A King in check by a piece (P1) "exposes" another piece (P3) when it is moved out of check to (X4,Y4)
pin	A piece (P3) cannot move because it will produce a check on its own side by piece (P1)

```
pin(S1,P1,(X1,Y1),S2,king,(X2,Y2),S2,P3,(X3,Y3),(X4,Y4),Pos1) :-
        sliding_piece(P1,(X1,Y1),Pos1),
        make_move(S1,P1,(X1,Y1),(X4,Y4),Pos1,Pos2),
        sliding_piece(P1,(X4,Y4),Pos2),
        stale(S2,P3,(X3,Y3),Pos2),
        threat(S1,P1,(X4,Y4),S2,P3,(X3,Y3),Pos2),
        in_line(S2,king,(X2,Y2),S2,P3,(X3,Y3),S1,P1,(X4,Y4),Pos2).
```

FIGURE 6.3 Modified PAL rule for the pin pattern to convert it into a tactic.

EVALUATION

We wish to investigate whether the synthesized tactics tend to suggest good moves to play. We do this by measuring coverage and divergence for each of our tactics over a set of positions using both a strong and a weak reference engine. For our strong reference engine, we use *Stockfish 14*, the winner of the TCEC 2020 Championship (Haworth & Hernandez 2021). For our weak reference engine, we use Maia Chess (McIlroy-Young et al. 2020), a chess engine trained to produce human-like moves. We use the maia1 model, which is targeted toward 1100 ELO (a measure of relative playing strength, and roughly equal to a beginner). We limit the search depth to one-ply for both Stockfish 14 and Maia 1100 to resemble our tactics. As a baseline, we use a random tactic which is applicable to all positions and produces a random legal move in the position. We limit the number of suggestions from a tactic to 3, and assume the output order of tactic suggestions as the intended ranked order. For ease of implementation, we manually translated the tactics from Prolog definitions to Python functions. We use 5,000 games from the January 2013 archive of standard rated games played on lichess.com (lichess.org 2021). For each game, we generate positions by iterating through the move list, making the move, and adding the resulting position to the evaluation set. In total, we generate 325,830 positions.

RESULTS AND ANALYSIS

We summarize the results of our evaluation in Table 6.2. From the high coverage values obtained, we conclude that tactics like *can_threat* and *discovered_threat* are too general, whereas tactics like *discovered_threat* are too specific. Tactics like *can_check, can_fork*, and *skewer* strike a balance between these extremes.

From the divergence metrics calculated using Maia 1100 (our weak engine), we see that most of our tactics have lower divergence scores than our random baseline, indicating that they tend to produce moves that are evaluated somewhat similarly to a weak engine's best moves. For Stockfish 14 (SF14), however, all our tactics have higher divergence scores than random, indicating that they do not tend to produce moves similar to a strong engine. Thus, we qualitatively conclude that our tactics resemble that of a beginner chess player.

PROPOSED EVALUATION

We propose an experiment to investigate whether the identified set of tactics are useful for a human player to learn in order to generate good moves. To do this, we will measure the win-rate of a chess engine against

TABLE 6.2 Coverage and DCG for Each Tactic

Tactic	**Coverage**	**Divergence**	
		SF14	**Maia**
can_threat	0.96	378.94	9.22
can_check	0.45	549.19	4.02
can_fork	0.32	676.45	4.67
discovered_check	≈0	338.55	18.64
discovered_threat	0.96	375.97	1.19
skewer	0.22	748.4	5.41
pin	0.79	526.45	4.9
random	**1**	**328.09**	**8.28**

a version of itself augmented with these tactics. As a human proxy, we plan to use Maia Chess, specifically the maia1 model targeted toward 1100 ELO. We will play games between the engines of 30 minutes + 5 seconds time control, following the TCEC League rules (kanchess 2021) and starting from the default start position. As before, we will limit the evaluation depth of the search tree for the augmented and un-augmented engines to 1. We measure the divergence scores for our tactics with a strong reference engine (Stockfish 14). We will modify the action-selection procedure of Maia Chess to utilize the first suggestion of the lowest divergence tactic applicable to a given position, instead of the engine's move choice. This is made explicit in Algorithm 1. Finally, we will compare the win rates of the augmented engine against the unmodified version of itself over multiple games. Our hypothesis is that the augmented engine will have significantly higher win rate, enabling us to conclude that the set of tactics tend to suggest good moves.

Algorithm 1: Augmented engine move selection

Input: Set of tactics T, position p, chess engine move selection procedure C.make_move($\cdot$)
Output: Legal move in position p
1: move $\leftarrow$ C.make_move(p)
2: min_divg $\leftarrow$ ∞
3: **for** $t \in T$ **do**
4: **if** t matches p **and** divg(t) $<$ min_divg **then**
5: move $\leftarrow$ t.suggestion
6: min_divg $\leftarrow$ divg(t)
7: **end if**
8: **end for**
9: **return** move

CONCLUSION AND FUTURE WORK

We have described a symbolic sub-policy model for chess inspired by the pattern-action model of chess tactics. We have used patterns learned by an ILP system to construct these tactics. We have contributed a metric for measuring the divergence of these tactics to a reference chess-playing agent. We evaluated a set of tactics learned by a chess pattern learning system using our metric to find that they resembled a weak engine, but were not similar to a strong one.

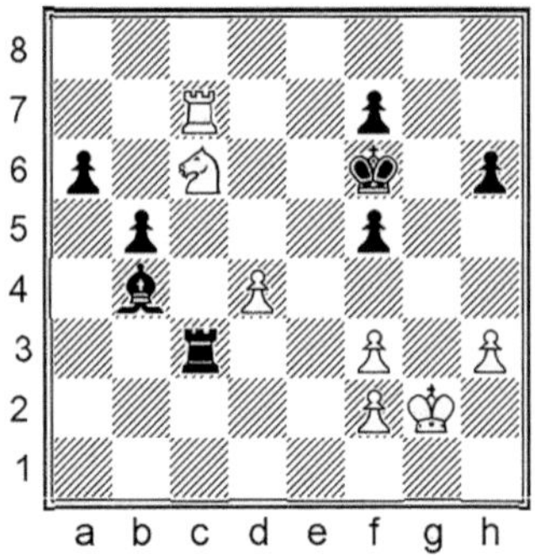

FIGURE 6.4 An example of the limitations of our one-ply *can_fork* tactic. White has no immediate forking move here, leading to the tactic not matching. However, if they play **1. Nxb4**, then Black's best response is **1 .... Rxc7** which allows a fork with **2. Nd5+** leading to the capture of the rook.

We use patterns learned by PAL to obtain our tactics. However, PAL uses manual labeling of generated examples to learn specific concepts, and requires additional effort to convert the learned patterns into tactics for our model. We aim to investigate the automatic learning of tactics from a data set of chess positions and move suggestions using ILP as implemented by modern systems like Popper (Cropper & Morel 2021). Future work could investigate alternate ILP algorithms (e.g., the δILP system (Evans & Grefenstette 2018)) that use our divergence metric as a loss function to optimize tactics.

Our tactic model is loosely inspired by how chess tactics are learned and practiced. However, our tactics are limited to looking 1-*ply* in the future (i.e., they can recognize only the presence of a matching pattern in the immediately next position). Many chess tactics suggest *combinations* of moves, a series of moves where the matching pattern shows up only in a particular sequence (see Figure 6.4). Extending the tactic model to express and recognize such combinations will be a useful avenue for future work. We also wish to investigate the expression of longer-term plans from chess literature like centre control and pawn structure using tactics.

Our appeal to the interpretability of these tactics rests on similar claims made regarding the interpretability of rule-based strategies. Future work will involve rigorously testing these assumptions with user studies using evidence-based measures of interpretability (Lage et al. 2019; Kliegr, Bahník, & Fürnkranz 2021). Specifically, we wish to investigate the ease of learning and applying these tactics in real games played by human players.

NOTE

1. Fruit fly; easily bred and thus extensively used in genetics research.

REFERENCES

Andrei, M. (2021). A supercomputer helped set up the World Chess Championship game. Accessed: 2021-10-27.

Bastani, O., Pu, Y., & Solar-Lezama, A. (2018). *Verifiable reinforcement learning via policy extraction.* arXiv preprint arXiv:1805.08328.

Benbassat, A., & Sipper, M. (2011). Evolving board-game players with genetic programming. In *Proceedings of the Thirteenth Annual Genetic and Evolutionary Computation Conference (Conference Companion)* (pp. 739 –742). ACM Press.

Berliner, H. J. (1975). *A representation and some mechanisms for a problem-solving chess program* (Technical report). Department of Computer Science, Carnegie-Mellon University.

Berner, C., Brockman, G., Chan, B., Cheung, V., Dębiak, P., Dennison, C., Farhi, D., Fischer, Q., Hashme, S., Hesse, C. & Józefowicz, R. (2019). *Dota 2 with large scale deep reinforcement learning.* arXiv preprint arXiv:1912.06680.

Bramer, M. A. (1977). *Representation of knowledge for chess endgames towards a self-improving system.* [Doctoral Dissertation, Open University (United Kingdom)].

Bratko, I. (1982). Knowledge-based problem-solving in AL3. *Machine Intelligence, 10*, 73–100.

Broll, B., Hausknecht, M., Bignell, D., & Swaminathan, A. (2019). Customizing scripted bots: Sample efficient imitation learning for human-like behavior in Minecraft. In *AAMAS Workshop on Adaptive and Learning Agents.*

Buntine, W. (1988). Generalized subsumption and its applications to induction and redundancy. *Artificial Intelligence, 36*(2), 149–176.

Butler, E., Torlak, E., & Popovic, Z. (2017). Synthesizing interpretable strategies for solving puzzle games. In *Proceedings of the Twelfth International Conference on the Foundations of Digital Games* (pp. 1–10). Hyannis, MA: ACM Press.

Canaan, R., Shen, H., Torrado, R., Togelius, J., Nealen, A., & Menzel, S. (2018). Evolving agents for the Hanabi 2018 CIG competition. In *Proceedings of the IEEE Conference on Computational Intelligence and Games* (pp. 1–8). IEEE Press.

Connors, M. H., Burns, B. D., & Campitelli, G. (2011). Expertise in complex decision making: the role of search in chess 70 years after de Groot. *Cognitive Science, 35*(8), 1567–1579.

Coppens, Y., Efthymiadis, K., Lenaerts, T., Nowé, A., Miller, T., Weber, R., & Magazzeni, D. (2019). Distilling deep reinforcement learning policies in soft decision trees. In T. Miller, R. Weber, D. Aha, & D. Magazzeni (Eds.) *Explainable Artificial Intelligence: Papers from the IJCAI Workshop.* [https://drive.google.com/file/d/1ma5wilaj31A0d5KC4I2fYaTC_Lqm_d9X/view].

Cropper, A. & Dumančić, S. (2020). *Inductive logic programming at 30: Aa new introduction.* arXiv preprint arXiv:2008.07912.

Cropper, A. & Morel, R. (2021). Learning programs by learning from failures. *Machine Learning, 110*(4), 801–856.

Derner, E., Kubalík, J., & Babuška, R. (2018). Data-driven construction of symbolic process models for reinforcement learning. In *Proceedings of the IEEE International Conference on Robotics and Automation* (pp. 5105–5112). IEEE Press.

de Freitas, J. M., de Souza, F. R., & Bernardino, H. S. (2018). Evolving controllers for Mario AI using grammar-based genetic programming. In *Proceedings of the Congress on Evolutionary Computation* (pp. 1–8). Rio de Janeiro: IEEE Press.

de Groot, A. D. (1946). *Het denken van den schaker: een experimenteel-psychologische studie.* Noord-Hollandsche Uitgevers Maatschappij Amsterdam.

Evans, R. & Grefenstette, E. (2018). Learning explanatory rules from noisy data. *Journal of Artificial Intelligence Research, 61*, 1–64.

Guid, M. & Bratko, I. (2006). Computer analysis of world chess champions. *ICGA Journal, 29*(2), 65–73.

Guid, M. & Bratko, I. (2011). Using heuristic-search based engines for estimating human skill at chess. *ICGA Journal, 34*(2), 71–81.

Haworth, G. & Hernandez, N. (2021). The 20th Top Chess Engine Championship. *ICGA Journal*, (Preprint), 1–12.

Huberman, B. J. (1968). *A program to play chess end games* (Technical Report 65). Department of Computer Science, Stanford University.

Järvelin, K. & Kekäläinen, J. (2002). Cumulated gain-based evaluation of IR techniques. *ACM Transactions on Information Systems, 20*(4), 422–446.

kanchess. 2021. TCEC Leagues Season Rules. Accessed: 2021-10-27.

Kliegr, T., Bahník, Š. & Fürnkranz, J. (2021). A review of possible effects of cognitive biases on interpretation of rule-based machine learning models. *Artificial Intelligence, 295*, 103458.

Lage, I., Chen, E., He, J., Narayanan, M., Kim, B., Gershman, S. J., & Doshi-Velez, F. (2019). Human evaluation of models built for interpretability. In *Proceedings of the Seventh AAAI Conference on Human Computation and Crowdsourcing* (pp. 59–67). Stevenson, WA: AAAI Press.

Landajuela, M., Petersen, B. K., Kim, S., Santiago, C. P., Glatt, R., Mundhenk, N., Pettit, J. F., & Faissol, D. (2021). Discovering symbolic policies with deep reinforcement learning. In *Proceedings of the 38th International Conference on Machine Learning* (pp. 5979–5989). PMLR 139.

Levinson, R. & Snyder, R. (1991). Adaptive pattern-oriented chess. In *Proceedings of the Eighth International Workshop on Machine Learning* (pp. 85–89). Evanston, IL: Morgan Kaufmann.

Li, J., Koyamada, S., Ye, Q., Liu, G., Wang, C., Yang, R., Zhao, L., Qin, T., Liu, T.-Y., & Hon, H.-W. (2020). *Suphx: Mastering mahjong with deep reinforcement learning.* arXiv preprint arXiv:2003.13590.

lichess.org (2021). lichess.org open database. https://database.lichess.org. Accessed: 2021-10-27.

Mariño, J. R. H., Rubens, O., Moraes, T. C., Oliveira, C. T., & Lelis, L. H. S. (2021). Programmatic strategies for real-time strategy games. In *Proceedings of the Thirty-Fifth AAAI Conference on Artificial Intelligence* (pp. 381–389). AAAI Press.

McCarthy, J. (1990). Chess as the drosophila of AI. In T. A. Marsland & J. Schaeffer (Eds.) *Computers, Chess, and Cognition*. New York, NY: Springer.

McGrath, T., Kapishnikov, A., Tomašev, N., Pearce, A., Hassabis, D., Kim, B., Paquet, U., & Kramnik, V. (2021). *Acquisition of chess knowledge in AlphaZero*. arXiv preprint arXiv:2111.09259.

McIlroy-Young, R., Sen, S., Kleinberg, J., & Anderson, A. (2020). Aligning superhuman AI with human behavior: Chess as a model system. In *Proceedings of the Twenty-Sixth ACM SIGKDD Conference on Knowledge Discovery and Data Mining* (pp. 1677–1687). ACM Press.

Moore, S., & Stamper, J. C. (2019). Exploring expertise through visualizing agent policies and human strategies in open-ended games. In *EDM (Workshops)*, 30–37.

Morales, E. (1992). *First order induction of patterns in Chess*. Ph.D. thesis, The Turing Institute, University of Strathclyde.

Osborn, J. C., Samuel, B., & Mateas, M. 2018. Visualizing the strategic landscape of arbitrary games. *Information Visualization, 17*(3), 196–217.

Pascutto, G.-C. & Linscott, G. (2019). Leela Chess Zero (v0.21.0).

Pitrat, J. (1977). A chess combination program which uses plans. *Artificial Intelligence, 8*(3), 275–321.

PTI. (2016). *World Chess Championship: Role of the 'seconds'* [Accessed: 2021-10-27]. [https://www.thehindu.com/sport/other-sports/world-chess-championship-role-of-the-seconds/article5313784.ece]

Puiutta, E. & Veith, E. M. (2020). Explainable reinforcement learning: A survey. In *Proceedings of the International Cross-Domain Conference for Machine Learning and Knowledge Extraction* (pp. 77–95). Springer.

Romero, O. (2019). Computer analysis of world chess championship players. *ICSEA 2019*, 212.

Romstad, T., Costalba, M., & Kiiski, J. (2021). Stockfish 14 [Computer software]. Retrieved from https://stockfishchess.org/blog/2021/stockfish-14/

Sadler, M., & Regan, N. (2019). *Game changer: AlphaZero's groundbreaking chess strategies and the promise of AI*. Alkmaar. The Netherlands: New in Chess.

Shannon, C. E. (1950). Programming a computer for playing chess. *The London, Edinburgh, and Dublin Philosophical Magazine and Journal of Science, 41*(314), 256–275.

Sieusahai, A. & Guzdial, M. (2021). Explaining deep reinforcement learning agents in the Atari domain through a surrogate model. In *Proceedings of the Seventeenth AAAI Conference on Artificial Intelligence and Interactive Digital Entertainment* (pp. 82–90). AAAI Press.

Silver, D., Huang, A., Maddison, C. J., Guez, A., Sifre, L., Van Den Driessche, G., Schrittwieser, J., Antonoglou, I., Panneershelvam, V., Lanctot, M. & Dieleman, S. (2016). Mastering the game of Go with deep neural networks and tree search. *Nature, 529*(7587), 484–489.

Silver, D., Hubert, T., Schrittwieser, J., Antonoglou, I., Lai, M., Guez, A., Lanctot, M., Sifre, L., Kumaran, D., Graepel, & Lillicrap, T. (2018). A general reinforcement learning algorithm that masters chess, shogi, and Go through self-play. *Science*, 362(6419), 1140–1144.

Smith, R. (2004). *Modern chess analysis*. Gambit. ISBN 9781904600084.

Spronck, P., Sprinkhuizen-Kuyper, I., & Postma, E. (2004). Online adaptation of game opponent AI with dynamic scripting. *International Journal of Intelligent Games and Simulation, 3*(1), 45–53.

Trivedi, D., Zhang, J., Sun, S.-H., & Lim, J. J. (2021). Learning to synthesize programs as interpretable and generalizable policies. *Advances in Neural Information Processing Systems, 34*, 25146–25163.

Tukmakov, V. (2020). *Modern chess formula: The powerful impact of engines*. Thinkers Publishing. ISBN 9789492510815.

Verma, A., Murali, V., Singh, R., Kohli, P., & Chaudhuri, S. (2018). Programmatically interpretable reinforcement learning. In *Proceedings of the Thirty-Fifth International Conference on Machine Learning* (pp. 5045–5054). PMLR 80.

Vinyals, O., Babuschkin, I., Czarnecki, W. M., Mathieu, M., Dudzik, A., Chung, J., Choi, D. H., Powell, R., Ewalds, T., Georgiev, P. & Oh, J. (2019). Grandmaster level in StarCraft II using multi-agent reinforcement learning. *Nature, 575*(7782), 350–354.

Wilkins, D. E. (1979). *Using patterns and plans to solve problems and control search*. Stanford University.

Wing, J. M. (2008). Computational thinking and thinking about computing. *Philosophical Transactions of the Royal Society A: Mathematical, Physical and Engineering Sciences, 366*(1881), 3717–3725.

Zhou, Y. (2018). Rethinking opening strategy: AlphaGo's impact on pro play. *CreateSpace, 1*(36), 212.

CHAPTER 7

The Need for Empirical Evaluation of Explanation Quality

Nicholas Halliwell[1], Fabien Gandon[1], Freddy Lecue[1,2], and Serena Villata[1]

[1]*Inria, Université Côte d'Azur, CNRS, France*
[2]*CortAIx, Thales, Montreal, Canada*

INTRODUCTION

Deep learning models are used to serve automated decisions in settings such as banks, insurance, and health care. These models are typically treated as a black box, where no insight is given as to how they make decisions. This lack of transparency has hindered adoption of these models into production. Much research has been devoted to developing algorithms, or explanation methods, to interpret their predictions.

Indeed, there are many approaches for generating post-hoc explanations. For example, feature importance methods (Lundberg & Lee 2017; Ribeiro, Singh, & Guestrin 2016; Kim et al. 2018) identify relevant dimensions and assign a score to rank their importance relative to the other dimensions. For image data, saliency maps (Simonyan, Vedaldi, & Zisserman 2014; Springenberg et al. 2015; Bach et al. 2015; Selvaraju et al. 2016; Shrikumar, Greenside, & Kundaje 2017; Shrikumar et al. 2016; Zeiler & Fergus 2014; Smilkov et al. 2017; Sundararajan, Taly, & Yan 2017; Montavon et al. 2017) identify relevant pixels in the input image. Counterfactual explanations (Wachter, Mittelstadt, & Russell 2017) determine the smallest possible perturbation to the given input that will

DOI: 10.1201/9781003355281-7

change the prediction to a desired target outcome. Lastly, prototype explanations (Chen et al. 2019; Li et al. 2018; Ming et al. 2019) learn a continuous vector that represents a "typical" training example, where explanations are given based on their relative distance to a prototype vector.

The prototype network architecture from Li et al. (2018) combines an autoencoder with a prototype layer, where each observation in the training set is classified based on its distance to a prototype vector. The encoded input from the autoencoder is used as features for predictions downstream. The prototype vectors learned by this network are defined as typical observations in the training set and, because they are learned in the same space as the encoded input, they can be mapped back into the original input space for visualization using the decoder.

Explanations are given in the form of a most similar prototype vector. The specific architecture of this network allows us to further develop and improve the types of explanations generated post hoc.

This chapter expands the type of explanations generated by the prototype network to identify relevant features in the input space. Due to the architecture of this network, the latent features learned by the model can be exploited to identify relevant input space features. We make use of the network's encoded input to randomly set latent features to zero, and use the network's decoder to determine which input space values changed the most. Finally, this work allows us to open a general discussion about generating explanations, identifying when one explanation method is preferable to another, and the complications that arise when measuring explanation quality.

PROTOTYPE NETWORK

This section provides necessary background information on the prototype network from Li et al. (2018), including the architecture and loss function.

ARCHITECTURE DETAILS

The prototype network architecture can be visualized in Figure 7.1. It consists of an autoencoder (the encoder defined as $f : R^p \rightarrow R^q$ and the decoder, defined as $g : R^q \rightarrow R^p$), a prototype layer $p : R^q \rightarrow R^m$, and a dense (fully connected) layer $w : R^m \rightarrow R^K$ that feeds into a softmax

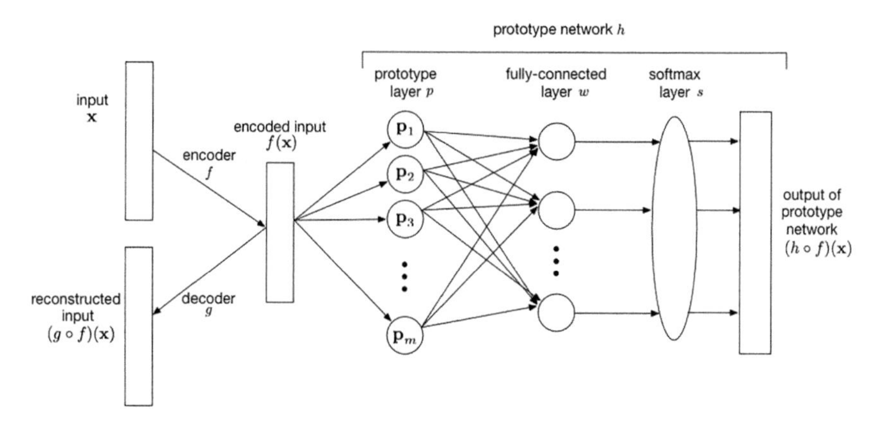

FIGURE 7.1 Prototype network architecture (Li et al. 2018).

layer. The prototype layer takes as input encoded training points, denoted $f(x_i)$, and computes the L^2 distance between $f(x_i)$ and m prototype vectors denoted $p_1, \ldots, p_m \in R^q$. The overall network is given by $h : R^q \rightarrow R^K$. In this prototype network architecture, observations are classified based on their distance to a prototypical observation, and the loss function ensures that each prototype vector is similar to an encoded training point. We denote the data set $D = \{(x_i, y_i)\}_{i=1}^{n}$, where $y_i \in \{1, \ldots, K\}$ and K being the number of classes.

LOSS FUNCTION

The loss function given by Li et al. (2018) is broken down into the following four parts below:

$$E(h \circ f, D) = \frac{1}{n} \sum_{i=1}^{n} \sum_{k=1}^{K} -1[y_i = k] \log((h \circ f)_k (x_i)) \tag{7.1}$$

$$R(g \circ f, D) = \frac{1}{n} \sum_{i=1}^{n} ||(g \circ f)(x_i) - x_i||_2 \tag{7.2}$$

$$R_1(p_1, \ldots, p_m, D) = \frac{1}{m} \sum_{j=1}^{m} min_{[i \in n]} ||p_j - f(x_i)||_2 \tag{7.3}$$

$$R_2(p_1, \ldots, p_m, D) = \frac{1}{n} \sum_{i=1}^{n} min_{[i \in m]} ||f(x_i) - p_j||_2 \tag{7.4}$$

The complete loss function is given by

$$L((f, g, h), D) = E(h \circ f, D) + \lambda_0 R(g \circ f, D) + \lambda_1 R_1(p_1, \ldots, p_m, D) + \lambda_2 R_2(p_1, \ldots, p_m, D) \quad (7.5)$$

where $\lambda_0, \lambda_1, \lambda_2$ are hyperparameters.

PROPOSED APPROACH

The encoder function f maps a p dimensional vector to a q dimensional vector where $p > q$. This encoded input contains relevant information for classification, as it is used as features downstream, and is using a lower-dimensional representation of the input data. Identifying relevant information in the encoded latent space should provide further insight into how the model is making decisions. For some observation x, we want an explanation for, we encode the input using the prototype network's encoder f. We then make m copies of the encoded input $f(x)$, and apply m different masks element-wise. Each mask, denoted m_i, is the same dimensions as the encoded input $f(x)$, where each element of a mask is assigned a 1 with 90% probability and a 0 with 10% probability. The element-wise product is then averaged across the m masks, given by:

$$\hat{f}(x) = \frac{1}{m} \sum_{i=1}^{m} f(x_i) \odot m_i \quad (7.6)$$

The result $\hat{f}(x)$ is then decoded by the prototype network's decoder g for visualization, given by:

$$\hat{g} = g(\hat{f}(x)) \quad (7.7)$$

To identify the relevant dimensions in the input space, the input is mapped through the encoder and then decoded, denoted $g(\hat{f}(x))$. We then compute the absolute difference between the decoded input and the decoded masked input given by:

$$x_* = |\hat{g} - g(f(x))| \quad (7.8)$$

where x^* gives the feature importance scores of x for each dimension. Here, the absolute difference gives the features in the input space with the largest change. The code for this chapter is available online.[1]

EXPERIMENTS

Image Data

With image data, we have the ability to visualize the explanation. We train a prototype network on the MNIST data set (LeCun et al. 1998) with three encoding layers, three decoding layers, one prototype layer, and one fully connected layer. This model learns ten prototype vectors (one for each class), achieving 99.1% accuracy on the test set.

Figure 7.3 shows saliency maps of the proposed approach for each image in Figure 7.2. We can see that the proposed approach produces saliency maps that outline the digit in the original image. We perform the model parameter randomization and data randomization test (Adebayo et al. 2018). The model parameter randomization test generates saliency maps from a model with untrained, random parameters. The resulting saliency maps should be random noise. The data randomization test trains a model where the training labels have been randomly shuffled. Like the model parameter randomization test, the resulting saliency maps should be random noise and the end user should not be able to determine the object in the image. Figure 7.4 shows

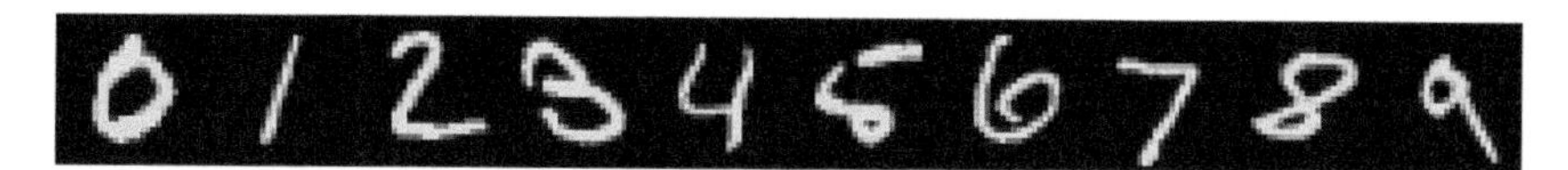

FIGURE 7.2 MNIST images.

FIGURE 7.3 Saliency maps: Proposed approach.

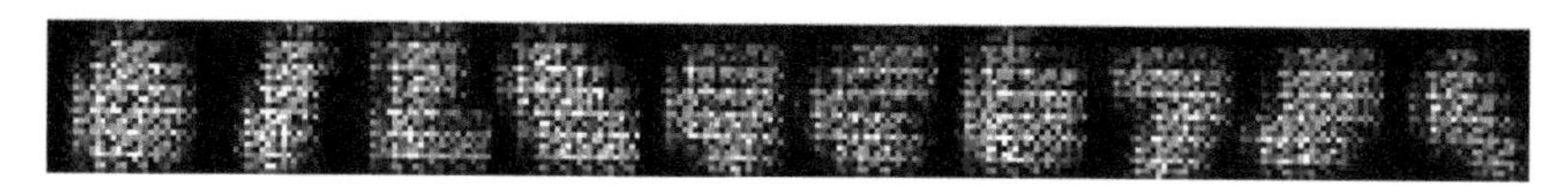

FIGURE 7.4 Saliency maps: Proposed approach-randomly initialized untrained network.

FIGURE 7.5 Saliency maps: Proposed approach-network trained on randomly permuted labels.

saliency maps from an untrained prototype network with randomly initialized parameters (model parameter randomization test). Figure 7.5 shows saliency maps for a model trained on random labels (data randomization test). From these figures, we can see the proposed approach passes the model parameter randomization test but fails the data randomization test. In other words, the proposed approach to generating explanations is not providing insight into what the model has learned.

Tabular Data

We demonstrate our approach on a well-known tabular data set, the California Housing data set (Pace & Barry, 1997). Here, we are tasked with determining if houses should be sold above or below the median price. We train a prototype network on the California Housing data set with two encoding layers, two decoding layers, one prototype layer, and one fully connected layer. This model learns two prototype vectors, achieving 84.2% accuracy on the test set.

Figure 7.6 compares relevant features identified by Lime (Ribeiro, Singh, & Guestrin 2016) to our proposed approach for selected observations. For both observations, we can see that the top three dimensions with the highest attribution scores are the same for both explanation methods. Although both explanations are similar, they are not exactly equal. From these examples, which explanation method is actually displaying what the model has learned? In other words, which explanation method is preferable to the other? These questions are difficult to answer without ground truth explanations to quantitatively compare against.

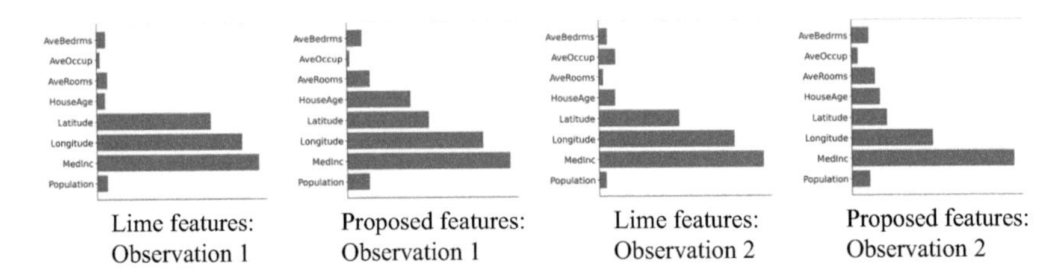

FIGURE 7.6 Explanations generated by Lime and the proposed approach on California Housing data set.

DISCUSSION

From the experiments on tabular and image data, we found our approach produced what looked like faithful explanations on both types of data. After using the robustness tests from Adebayo et al. (2018) on an image data set, we were able to determine that this was not the case. For image data, we have the ability to visually verify any explanation generated in the input space. With tabular data, we do not have this luxury. Depending on the type of data used for experimentation, researchers can be misled into thinking the explanations their model is generating are faithful because they are similar to a state-of-the-art method. With ground truth explanations, researchers would not have to rely on previous state-of-the-art explanation methods to determine if their approach is generating faithful explanations.

In general, this is a common problem in the field of XAI. When a new explanation method is proposed, researchers often show several "good looking" examples to display to the reader the capability of the proposed method. Comparisons against a state-of-the-art method typically involve a small number of cherry-picked examples to demonstrate the ability of an explanation method. This can be misleading. Indeed, a small number of selected examples do not truly represent how the explanation method is performing on the entire test set. As we demonstrated on the tabular data set, our proposed approach can compete with Lime on "selected" examples. However, this is not conclusive evidence that this explanation method is preferable to Lime. In order to accurately determine which explanation method is preferable, ground truth explanations are needed. In this chapter, we propose an explanation method for the sole purpose of demonstrating that the current standard for developing explanation methods does not rigorously evaluate the quality of explanations produced. This can lead to explanation methods producing explanations that do not truly reflect what the model has learned.

Defining ground truth explanations may be more difficult for different tasks, and different types of data. Additionally, there may be more than one way to explain a particular observation. Data sets with ground truth explanations must include all possible ways to explain each observation. Failing to include all possible ground truth explanations can unfairly penalize an explanation method for identifying a correct explanation not included in the ground truths.

There is existing work on qualitative evaluation of explanations. Poursabzi-Sangdeh et al. (2021) perform a user experiment to determine what makes a model interpretable. Jeyakumar et al. (2020) perform a user experiment to determine what style of explanation is preferred by users. Adebayo et al. (2020) develop a series of debugging tests, and include a user experiment to determine if users can identify defective models. Not much existing research focuses on quantitatively evaluating all test set explanations for quantitative comparisons across explanation methods. Relying on users to evaluate each explanation in the test set does not scale to large data sets, and cannot be performed on certain types of data (tabular data for example, users shown an explanation would not know if it is an accurate explanation or not). Additionally, users without a background in machine learning may not be able to determine a good explanation. For quantitative evaluations of explanations that scales to large data sets, scoring metrics must be defined that give an accurate representation of the explanation method's performance. Scoring metrics that measure explanation quality can be formally defined with ground truth explanations. Recently, researchers have proposed several data sets with ground truth explanations. For example, this includes the Royalty-20k and Royalty-30k data sets (Halliwell, Gandon, & Lecue 2021a) and the FrenchRoyalty-200k data set (Halliwell, Gandon, & Lecue 2021b), which were proposed along with several scoring metrics to quantitatively evaluate explanations. These data sets are Knowledge Graphs; they are limited to evaluating explanation methods of link prediction models on Knowledge Graphs.

CONCLUSION

In this chapter, we proposed a method to expand prototype networks to identify relevant features in the input space. We compared selected examples against a state-of-the-art explanation method on tabular data and verified that the explanations are similar. On image data, however, our approach passes the model parameter randomization test but fails the data randomization test. It is common practice in the field of XAI to compare explanation methods using a few selected examples. This is not a thorough evaluation of explanation quality.

We discussed the development of explanation methods, identifying when one explanation method is preferable to another, and the complications that arise when measuring explanation quality. Much research in the field of XAI is devoted to developing new explanation methods. This chapter points out that more work should be devoted to evaluating the quality of explanation generated. Many of these issues can be solved with ground truth explanations. We recognize this can be difficult with tabular data. Research should be devoted to defining ground truth explanations for all domains in order to quantitatively evaluate explanations.

NOTE

1. https://github.com/halliwelln/prototype-explanations.

REFERENCES

Adebayo, J., Gilmer, J., Muelly, M., Goodfellow, I. J., Hardt, M., & Kim, B. (2018). Sanity Checks for Saliency Maps. In S. Bengio, H. M. Wallach, H. Larochelle, K. Grauman, N. Cesa-Bianchi, & R. Garnett (Eds.), *Advances in Neural Information Processing Systems* 31.

Adebayo, J., Muelly, M., Liccardi, I., & Kim, B. (2020). Debugging Tests for Model Explanations. In H. Larochelle, M. Ranzato, R. Hadsell, M. F. Balcan, & H. Lin (Eds.), *Advances in Neural Information Processing Systems*. Curran Associates, Inc.

Bach, S., Binder, A., Montavon, G., Klauschen, F., Muller, K.-R., & Samek, W. (2015). On Pixel-Wise Explanations for Non-Linear Classifier Decisions by Layer-Wise Relevance Propagation. *PLOS ONE.*

Chen, C., Li, O., Tao, D., Barnett, A., Rudin, C., & Su J. (2019). This Looks Like That: Deep Learning for Interpretable Image Recognition. In H. M. Wallach, H. Larochelle, A. Beygelzimer, F. d'Alché-Buc, E. B. Fox, & R. Garnett (Eds.), *Advances in Neural Information Processing Systems* 32.

Halliwell, N., Gandon, F., & Lecue, F. (2021a). Linked Data Ground Truth for Quantitative and Qualitative Evaluation of Explanations for Relational Graph Convolutional Network Link Prediction on Knowledge Graphs. In *International Conference on Web Intelligence and Intelligent Agent Technology*. Melbourne, Australia.

Halliwell, N., Gandon, F., & Lecue, F. (2021b). User Scored Evaluation of Non-Unique Explanations for Relational Graph Convolutional Network Link Prediction on Knowledge Graphs. In *International Conference on Knowledge Capture*. Virtual Event, United States.

Jeyakumar, J. V., Noor, J., Cheng, Y., Garcia, L., & Srivastava, M. B. (2020). How Can I Explain This to You? An Empirical Study of Deep Neural Network Explanation Methods. In H. Larochelle, M. Ranzato, R. Hadsell, M. Balcan, & H. Lin (Eds.), *Advances in Neural Information Processing Systems* 33.

Kim, B., Wattenberg, M., Gilmer, J., Cai, C. J., Wexler, J., Viégas, F. B., & Sayres, R. (2018). Interpretability Beyond Feature Attribution: Quantitative Testing with Concept Activation Vectors (TCAV). In J. G. Dy & A. Krause (Eds.), *Proceedings of the 35th International Conference on Machine Learning, ICML 2018, Stockholm, Sweden, Proceedings of Machine Learning Research. PMLR.*

LeCun, Y., Bottou, L., Bengio, Y., & Haffner, P. (1998). Gradient-based learning applied to document recognition. *Proceedings of the Institute of Radio Engineers.*

Li, O., Liu, H., Chen, C., & Rudin, C. (2018). Deep Learning for Case-Based Reasoning Through Prototypes: A Neural Network That Explains Its Predictions. In S. A. McIlraith & K. Q. Weinberger (Eds.), *Proceedings of the Thirty-Second AAAI Conference on Artificial Intelligence.* AAAI Press.

Lundberg, S. M., & Lee, S. (2017). A Unified Approach to Interpreting Model Predictions. In I. Guyon, U. von Luxburg, S. Bengio, H. M. Wallach, R. Fergus, S. V. N. Vishwanathan, & R. Garnett (Eds.), *Advances in Neural Information Processing Systems* 30.

Ming, Y., Xu, P., Qu, H., & Ren, L. (2019). Interpretable and Steerable Sequence Learning via Prototypes. In A. Teredesai, V. Kumar; Y. Li, R. Rosales, E. Terzi, & G. Karypis (Eds.), *Proceedings of the 25th ACM SIGKDD International Conference on Knowledge Discovery & Data Mining, KDD 2019.* ACM.

Montavon, G., Lapuschkin, S., Binder, A., Samek, W., & Muller, K. (2017). Explaining nonlinear classification decisions with deep Taylor decomposition. Pattern Recognition Pace, R. K.; and Barry, R. 1997. Sparse spatial autoregressions. *Statistics & Probability Letters, 33,* 291.

Poursabzi-Sangdeh, F., Goldstein, D. G., Hofman, J. M., Vaughan, J. W., & Wallach, H. M. (2021). Manipulating and Measuring Model Interpretability. In Y. Kitamura, A. Quigley, K. Isbister, T. Igarashi, P. Bjørn, & S. M. Drucker (Eds.), *CHI '21: CHI Conference on Human Factors in Computing Systems.* ACM.

Ribeiro, M. T., Singh, S., & Guestrin, C. (2016). "Why Should I Trust You?": Explaining the Predictions of Any Classifier. In B. Krishnapuram, M. Shah, A. J. Smola, C. C. Aggarwal, D. Shen, & R. Rastogi (Eds.), *Proceedings of the 22nd ACM SIGKDD International Conference on Knowledge Discovery and Data Mining.* ACM.

Selvaraju, R. R., Das, A., Vedantam, R., Cogswell, M., Parikh, D., & Batra, D. (2016). Grad-CAM: Why did you say that? Visual Explanations from Deep Networks via Gradient-based Localization. CoRR, abs/1610.02391.

Shrikumar, A., Greenside, P., Shcherbina, A., & Kundaje A. (2016). Not Just a Black Box: Learning Important Features Through Propagating Activation Differences. CoRR abs/1605.01713.

Shrikumar, A., Greenside, P., & Kundaje, A. (2017). Learning Important Features Through Propagating Activation Differences. In (Precup and Teh 2017).

Simonyan, K., Vedaldi, A., & Zisserman, A. (2014). Deep Inside Convolutional Networks: Visualising Image Classification Models and Saliency Maps. In Y. Bengio & Y. LeCun (Eds.), *2nd International Conference on Learning Representations, ICLR 2014, Workshop Track Proceedings.*

Smilkov, D., Thorat, N., Kim, B., Viégas, F. B., & Wattenberg, M. (2017). SmoothGrad: removing noise by adding noise. CoRR, abs/1706.03825.

Springenberg, J. T., Dosovitskiy, A., Brox, T., & Riedmiller, M. A. (2015). Striving for Simplicity: The All Convolutional Net. In Y. Bengio & Y. LeCun (Eds.), *3rd International Conference on Learning Representations, ICLR 2015, Workshop Track Proceedings*.

Sundararajan, M., Taly, A., & Yan, Q. (2017). Axiomatic Attribution for Deep Networks. In (Precup and Teh 2017).

Wachter, S., Mittelstadt, B. D., & Russell, C. (2017). Counterfactual Explanations without Opening the Black Box: Automated Decisions and the GDPR. CoRR, abs/1711.00399.

Zeiler, M. D., & Fergus, R. (2014). Visualizing and Understanding Convolutional Networks. In D. J. Fleet, T. Pajdla, B. Schiele, & T. Tuytelaars (Eds.), *Computer Vision – ECCV 2014 – 13th European Conference, Lecture Notes in Computer Science*. Springer. ISBN 978-3-319-10589-5.

Index